ANGELS & WINGED BEINGS

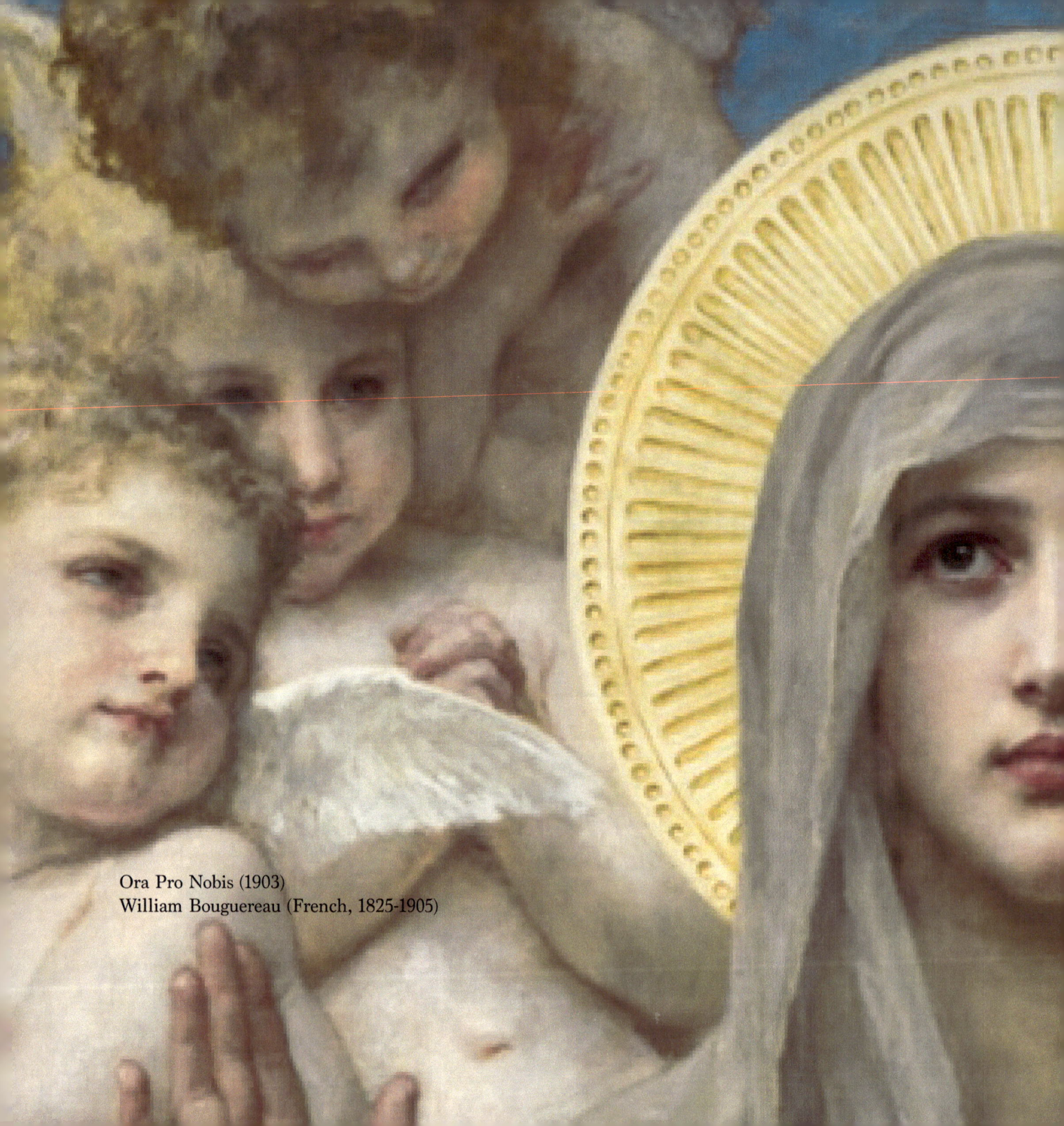

Ora Pro Nobis (1903)
William Bouguereau (French, 1825-1905)

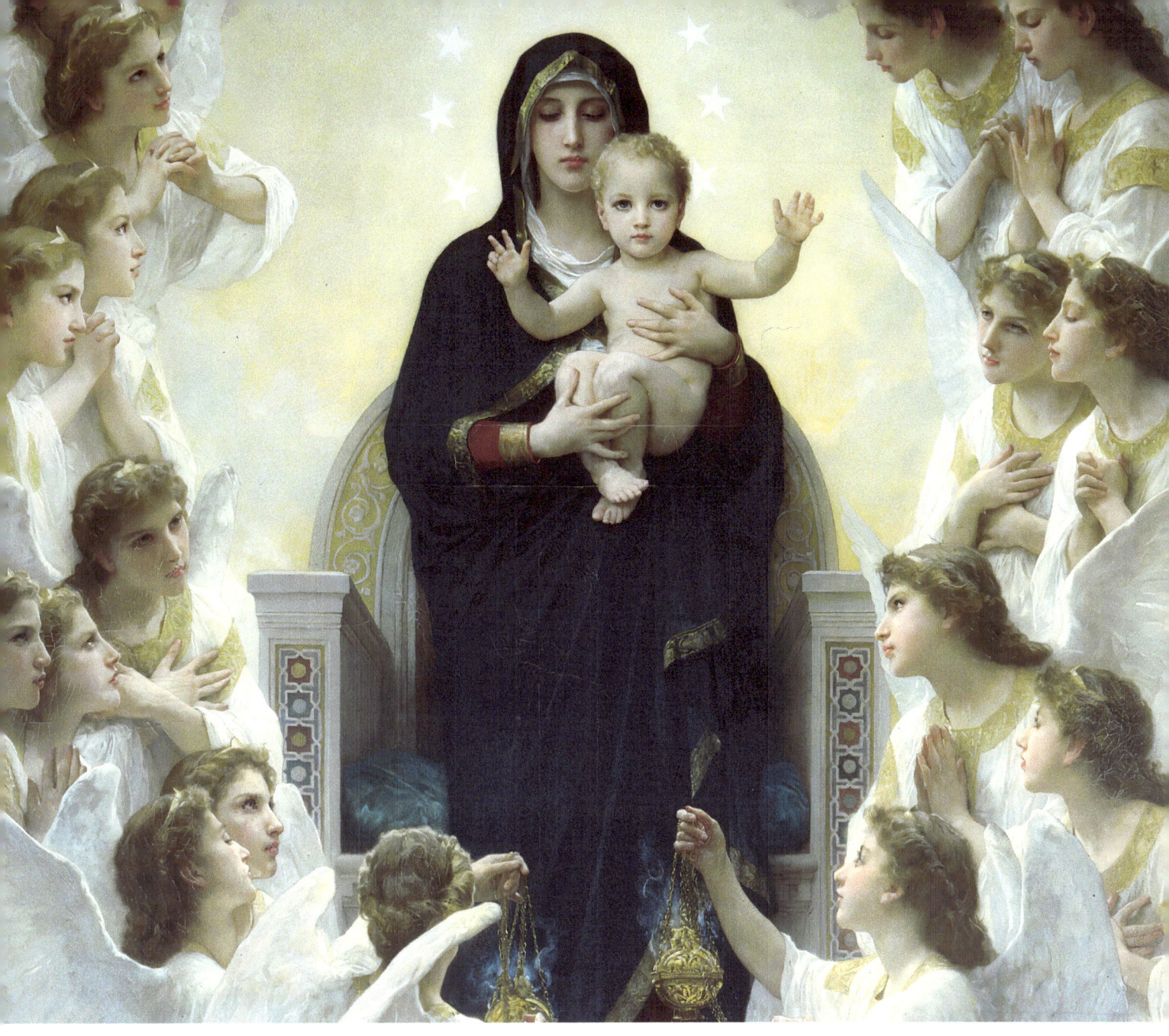

The Virgin With Angels (1900)
William Bouguereau (French, 1825-1905)

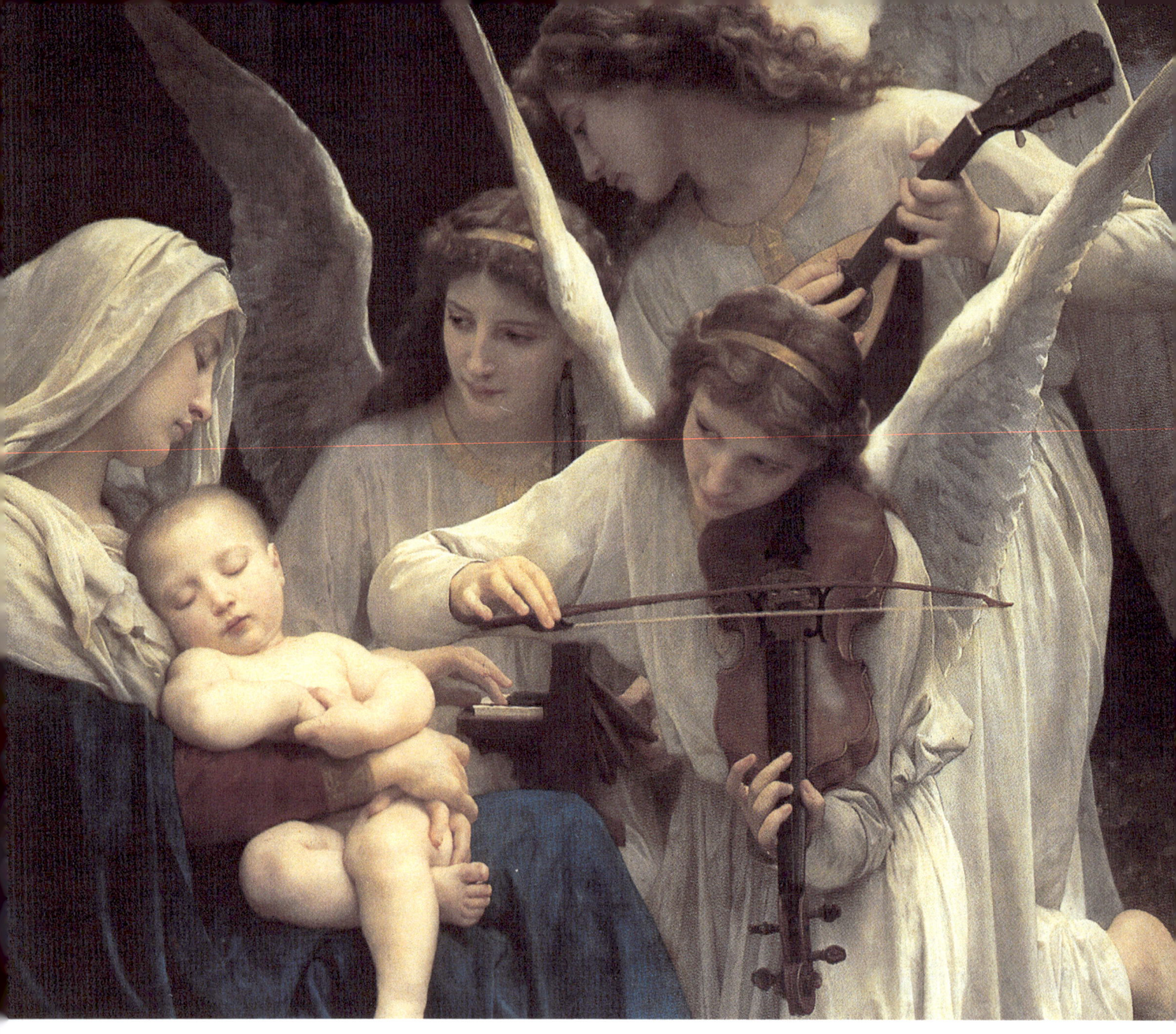

The song of the angels (1881)
William Bouguereau (French, 1825-1905)

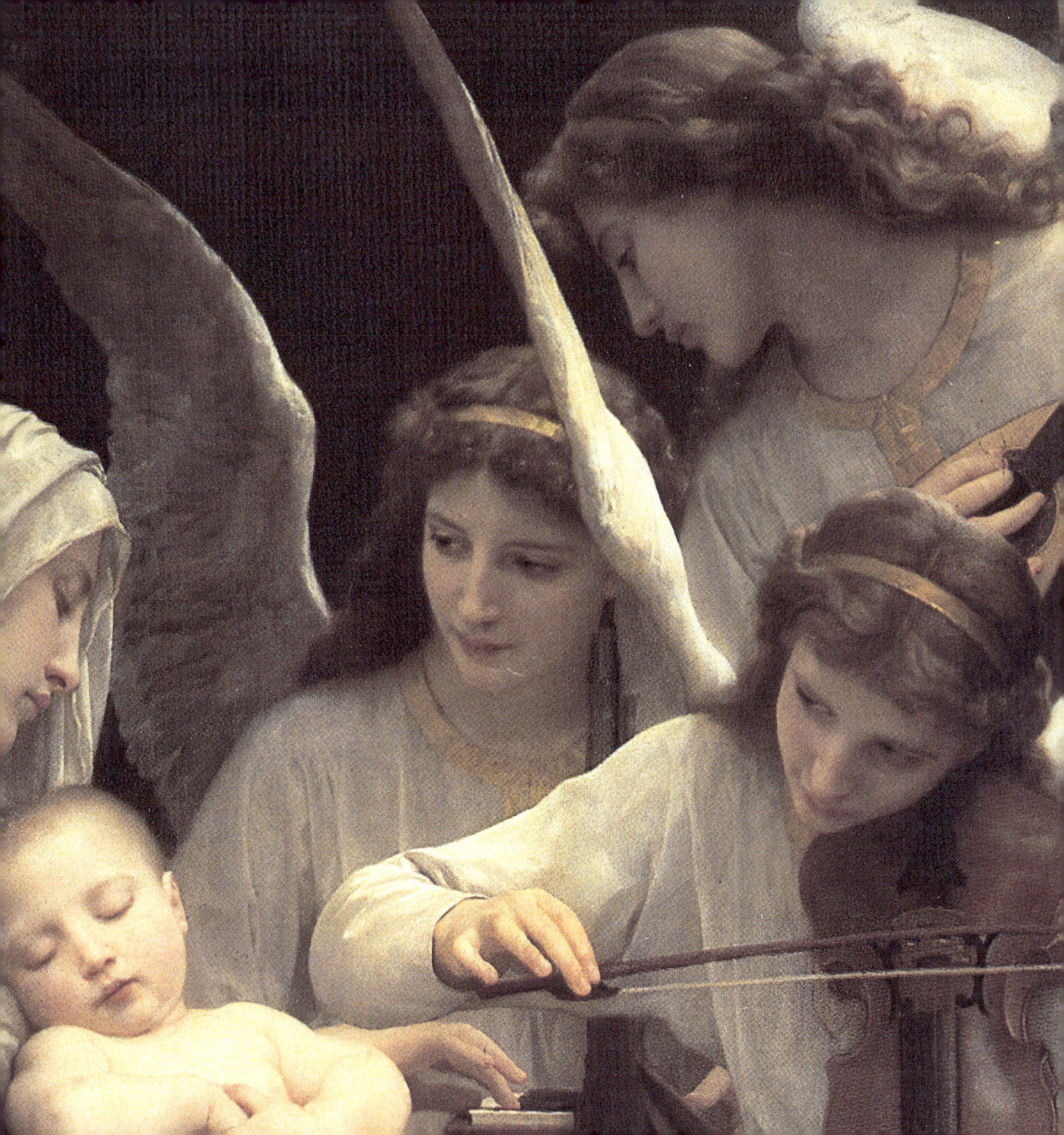

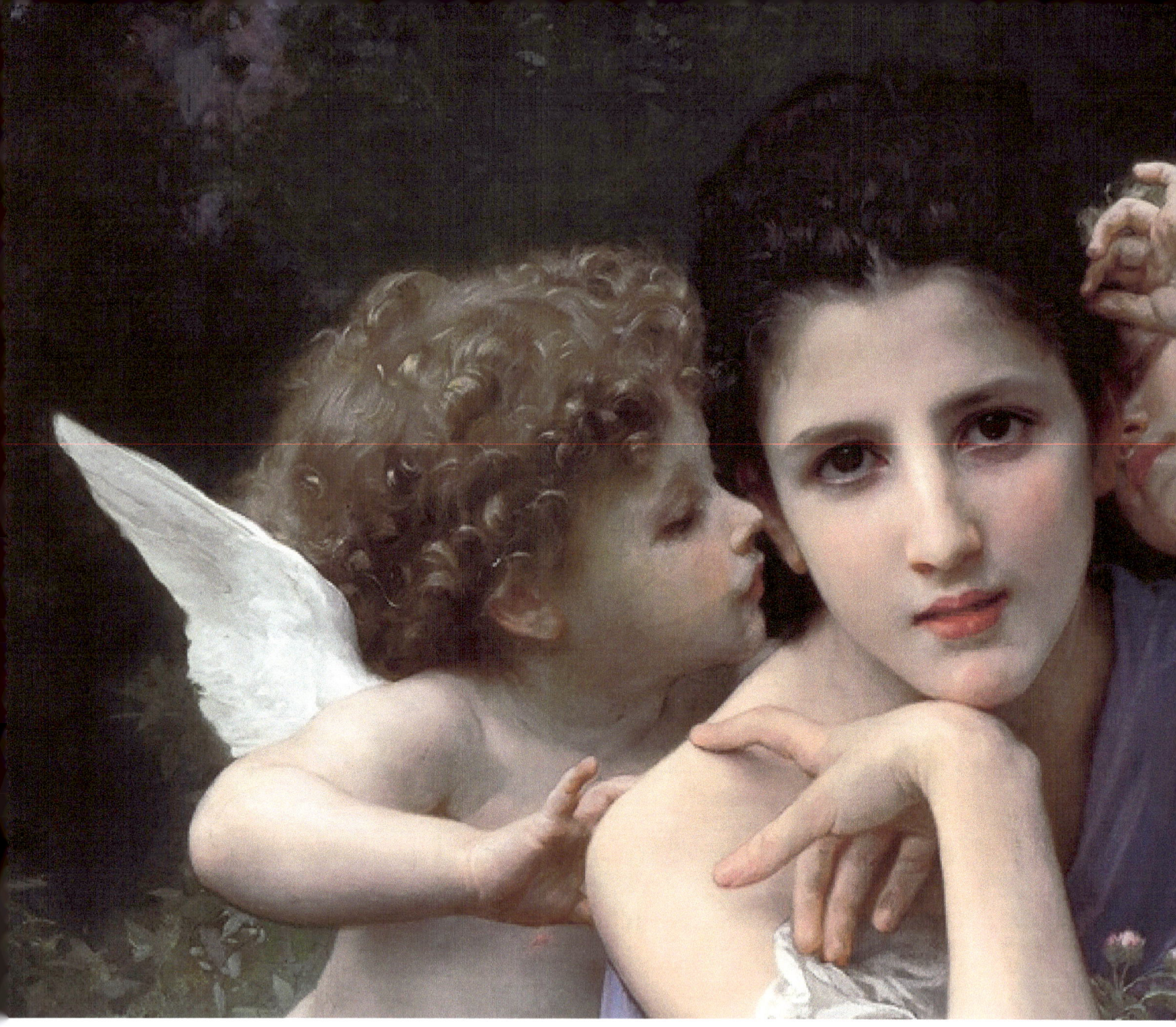

Chansons de printemps (1889)
William Bouguereau (French, 1825-1905)

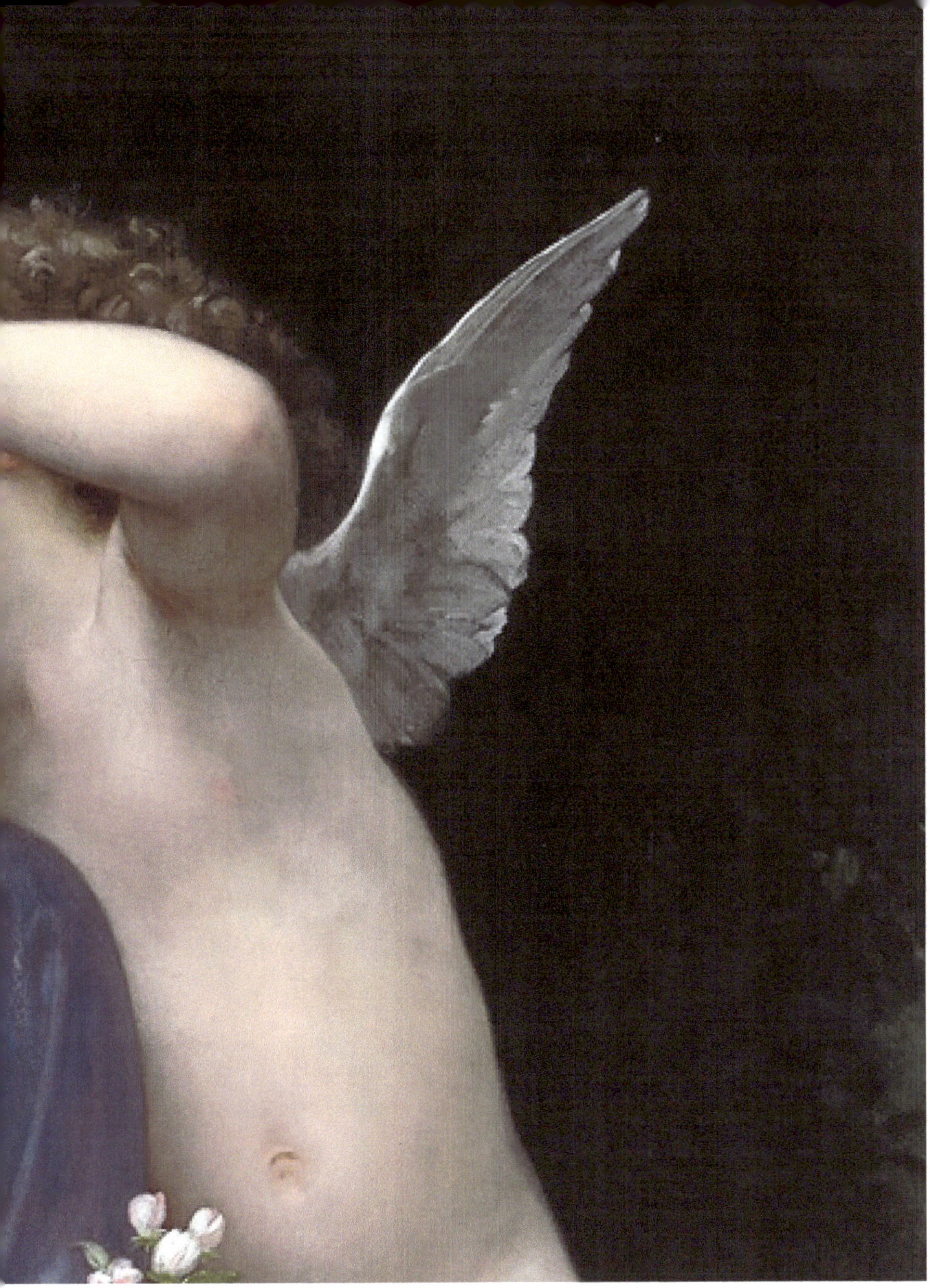

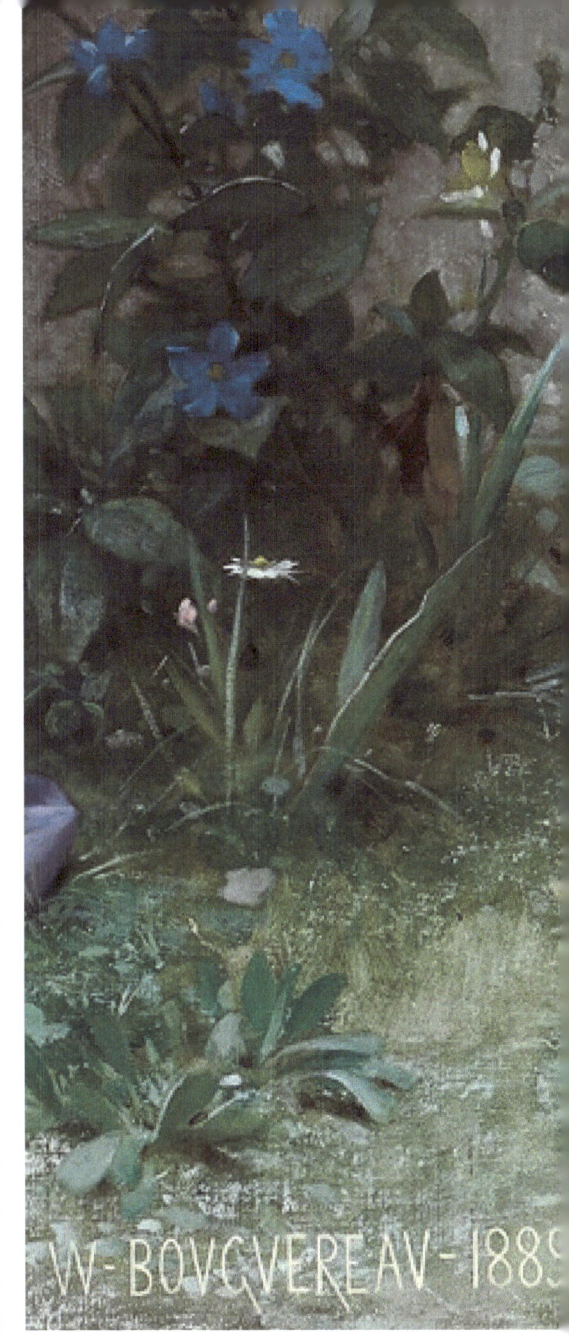

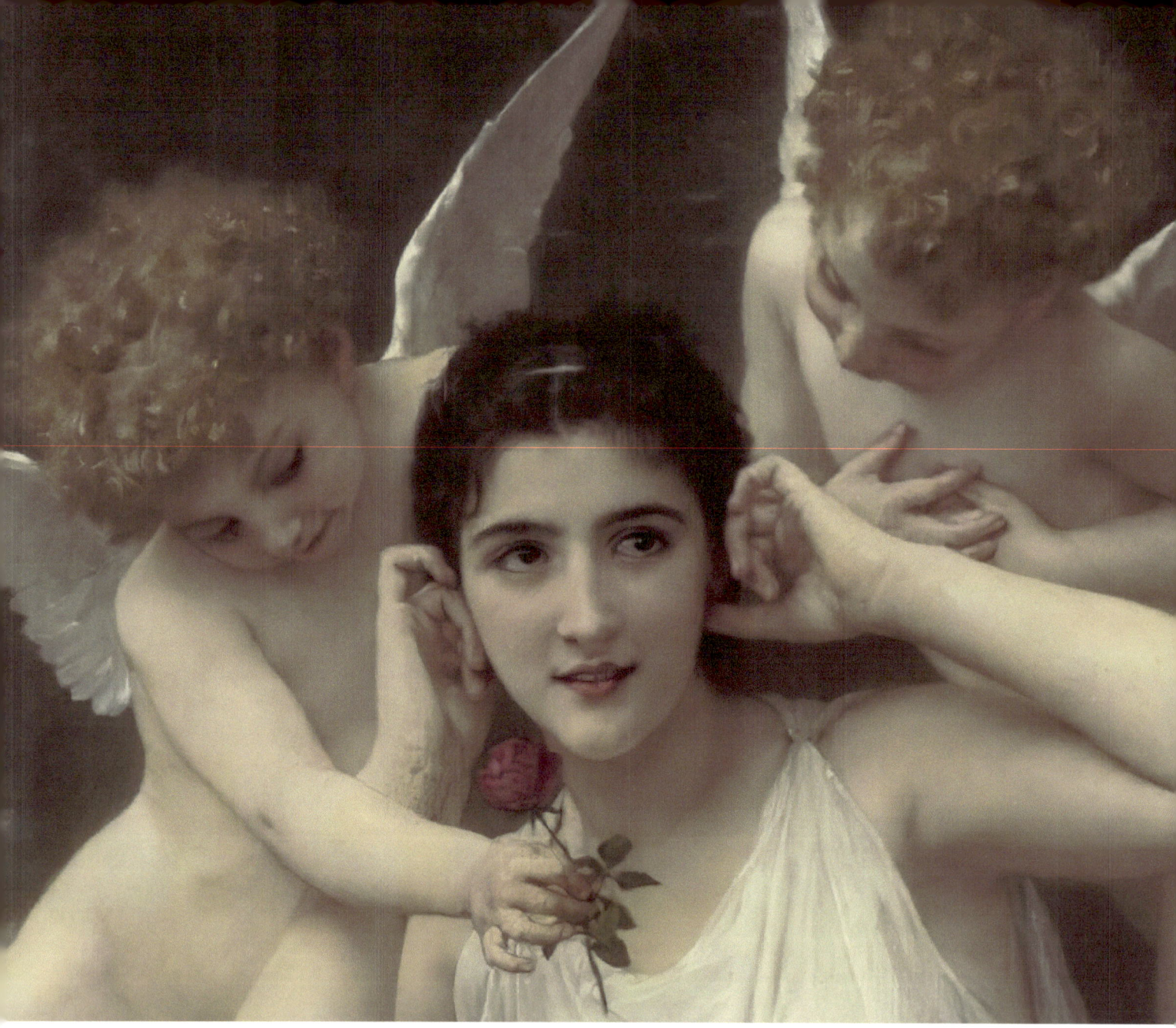

Bouquet of Roses in a Vase
Eugene Petit (French, 1839–1886)

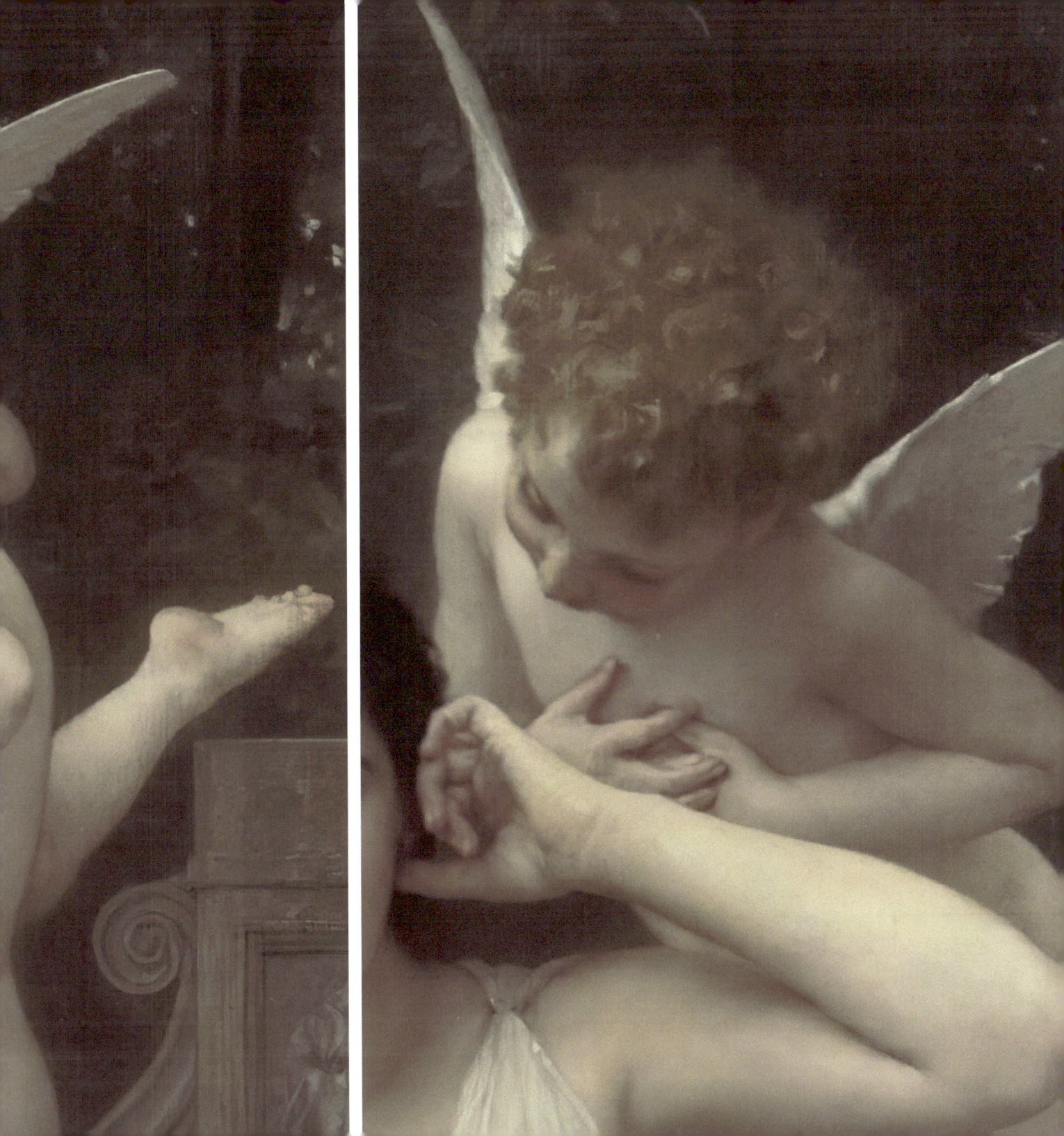

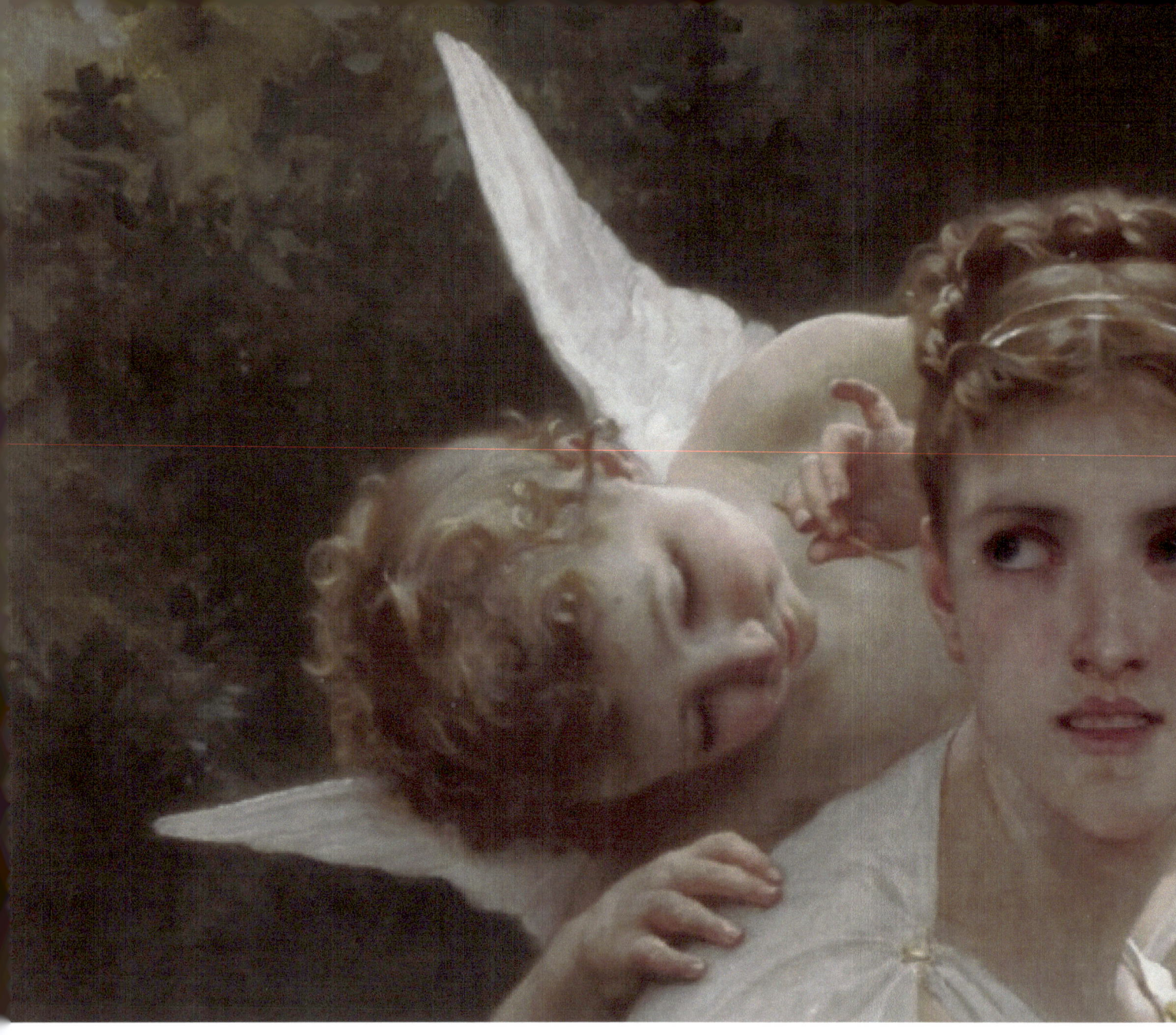

A Forest Floor with Roses and a Butterfly
Josef Lauer (Austrian, 1818–1881)

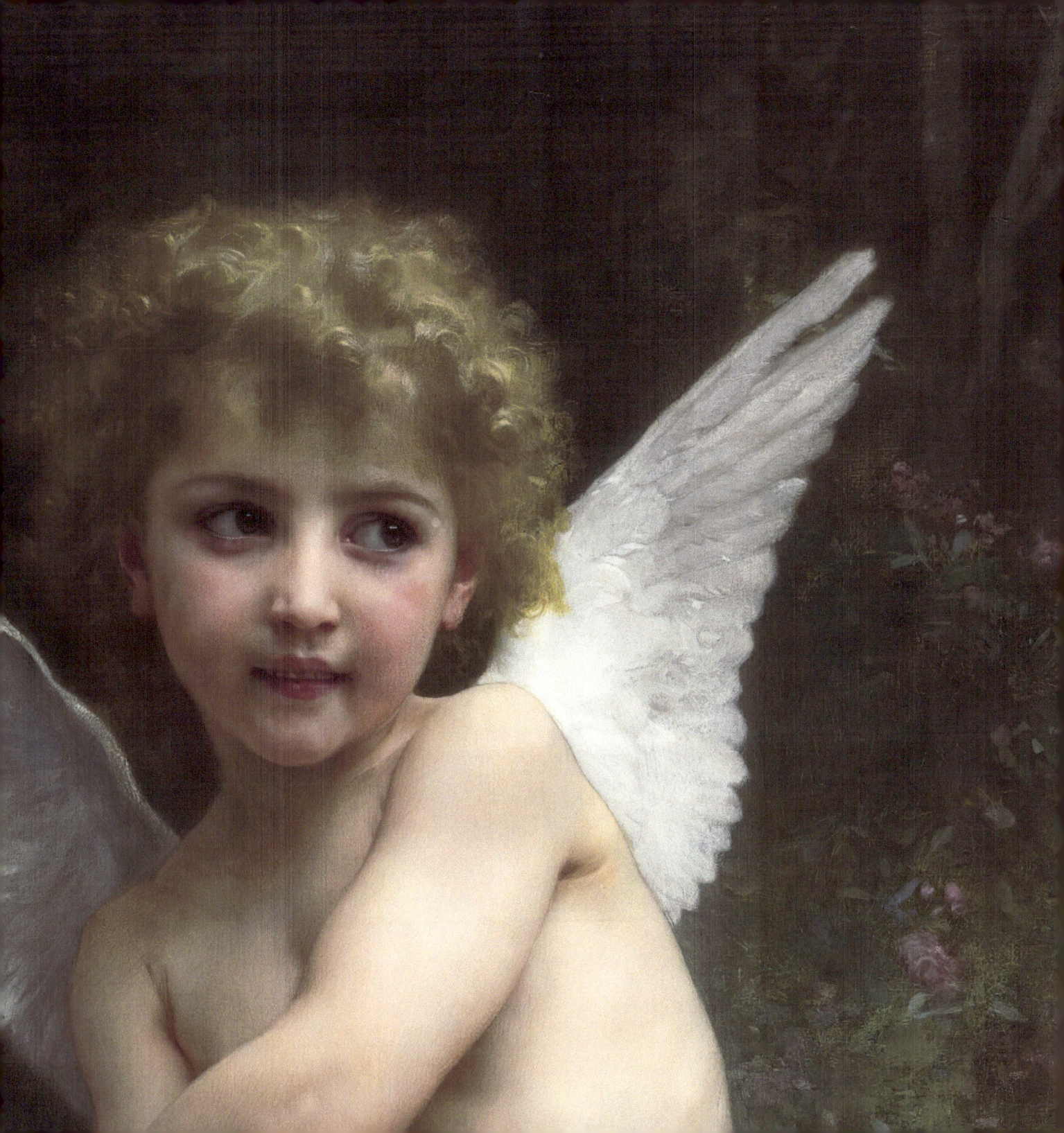

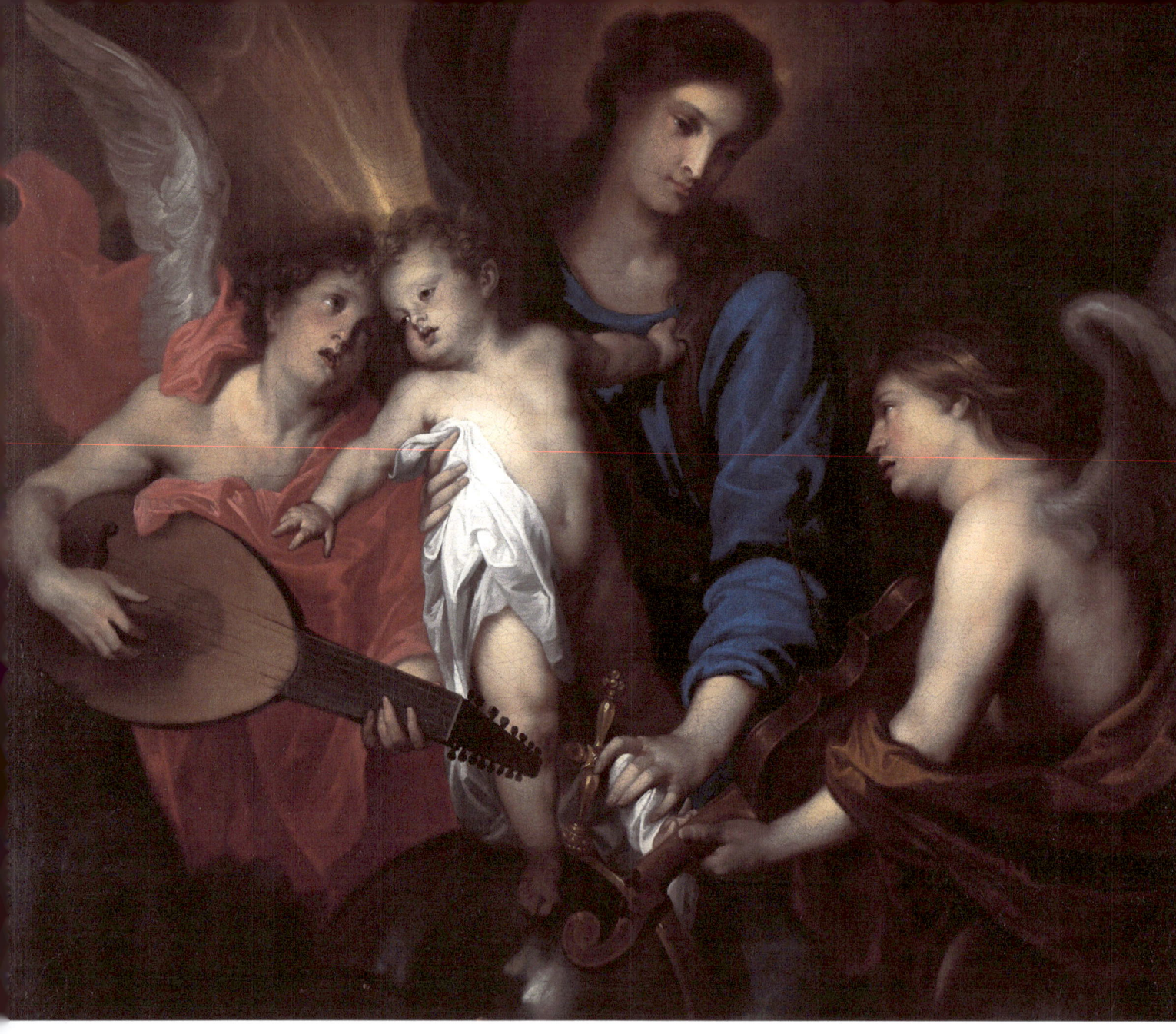

Virgin and Child with Music-Making Angels (ca. 1630)
Anthony van Dyck (Flemish, 1599-1641)

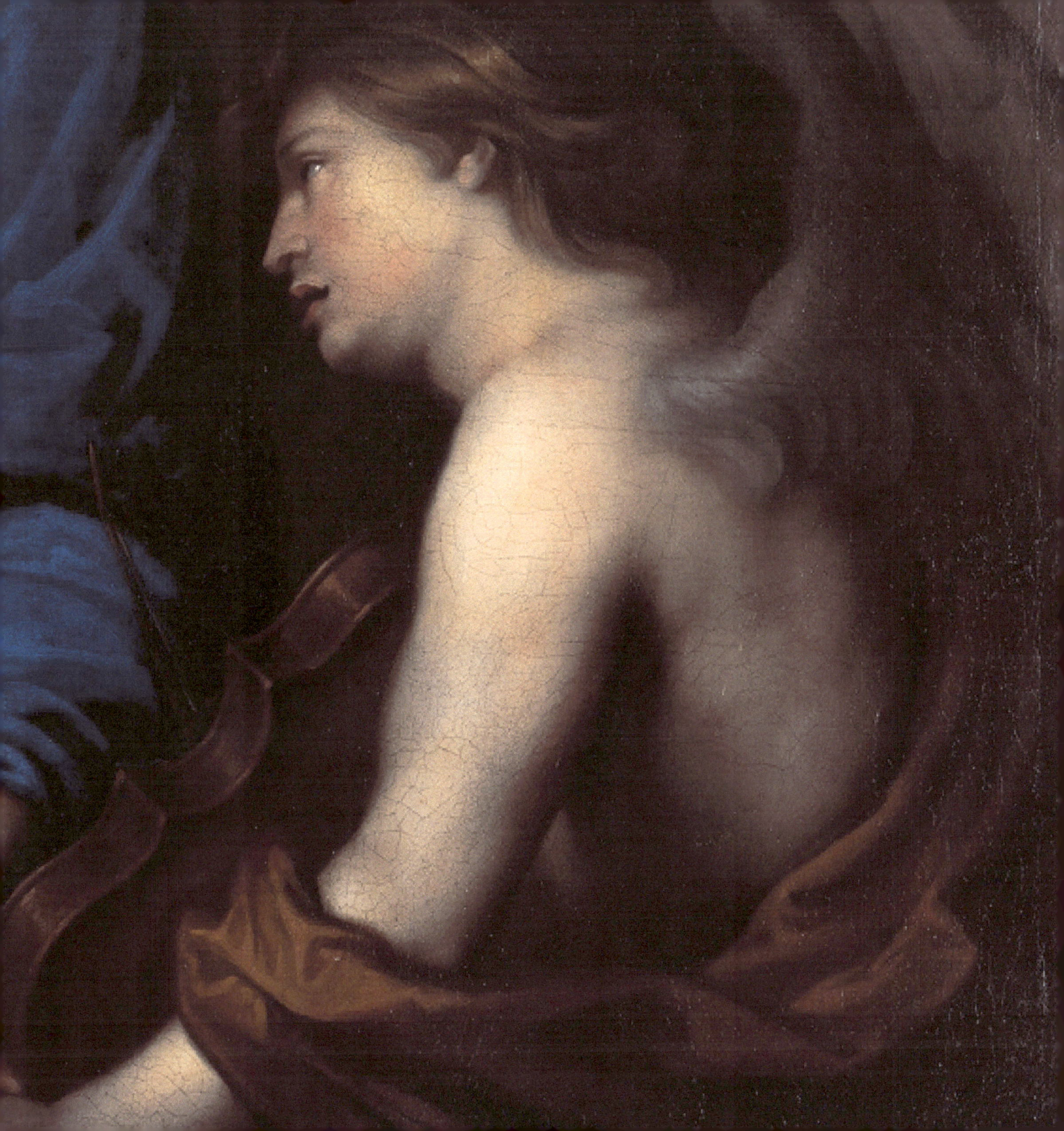

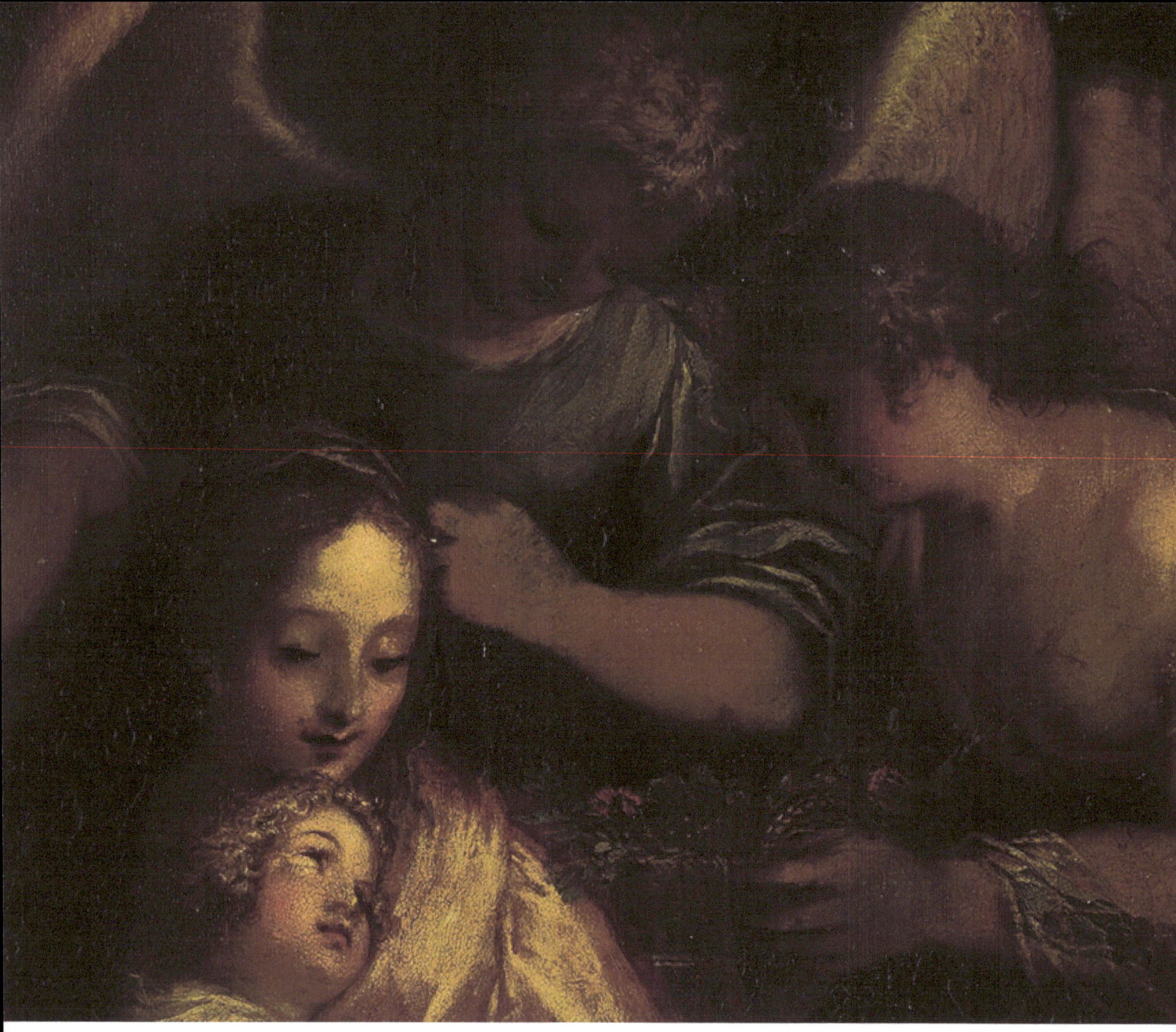

Madonna and child surrounded by angels
Hans Rottenhammer (German, 1564 – 1625)

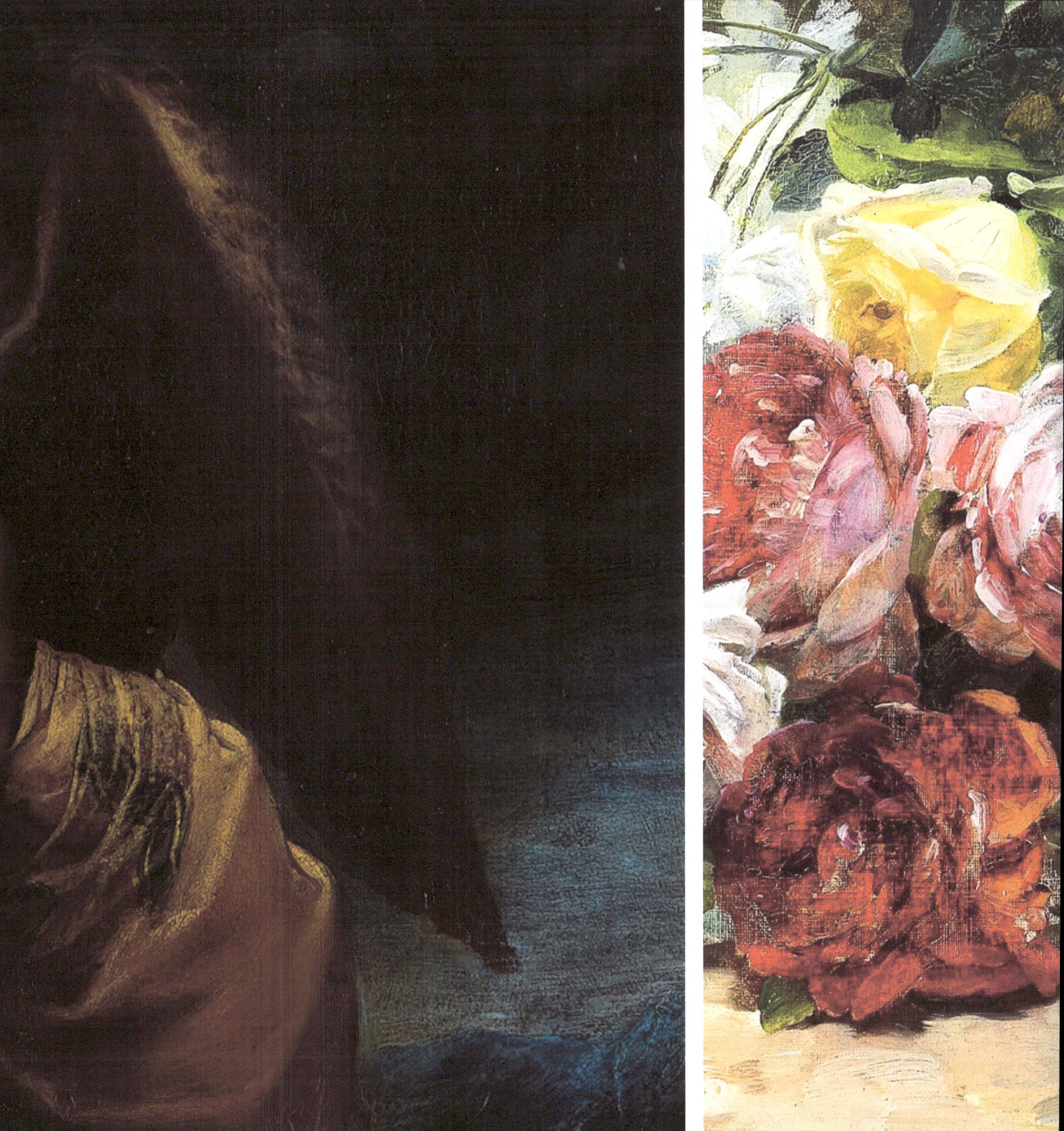

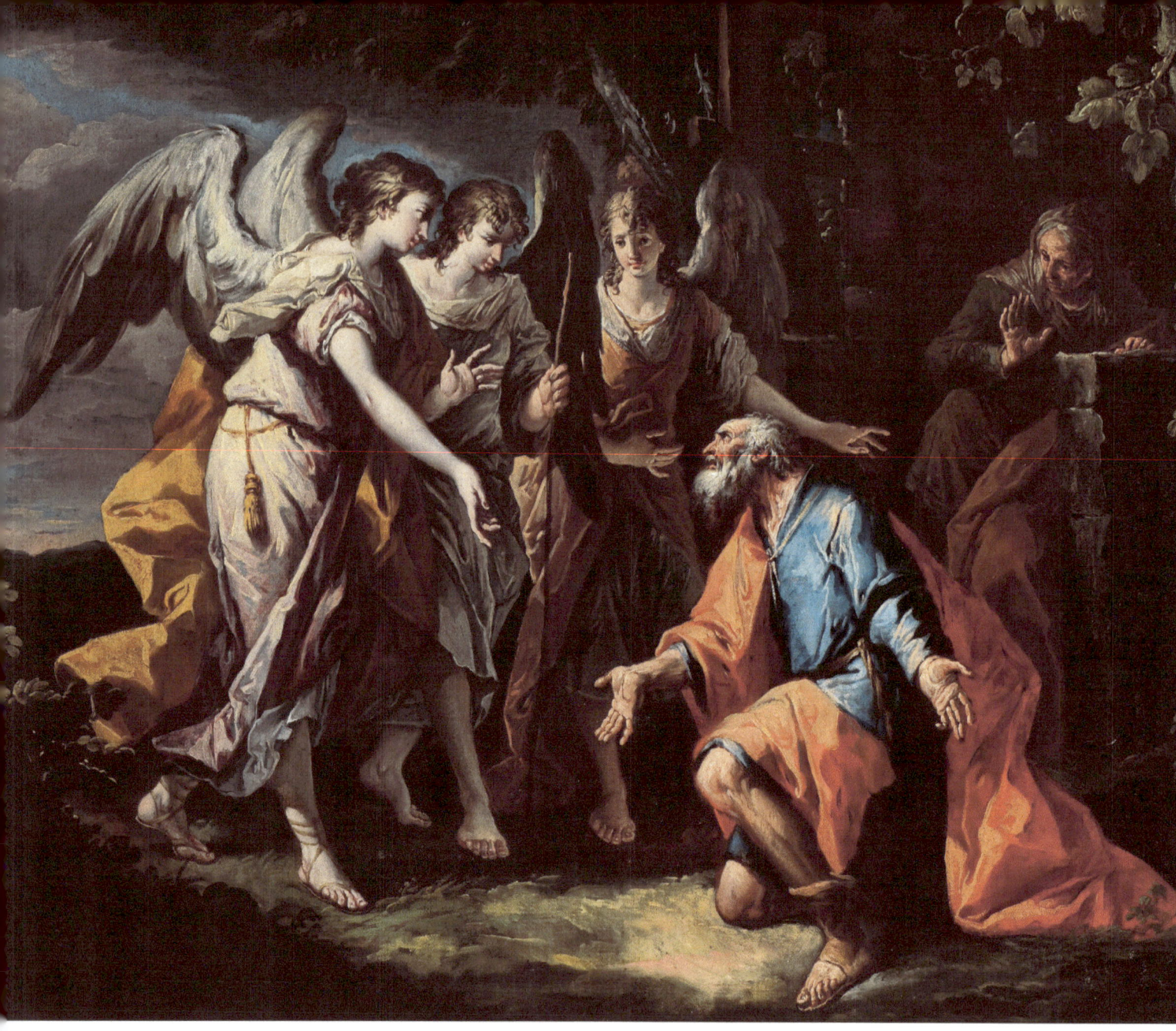

Abraham and the Angels (1735-1740)
Gaspare Diziani (Italian, 1689-1767)

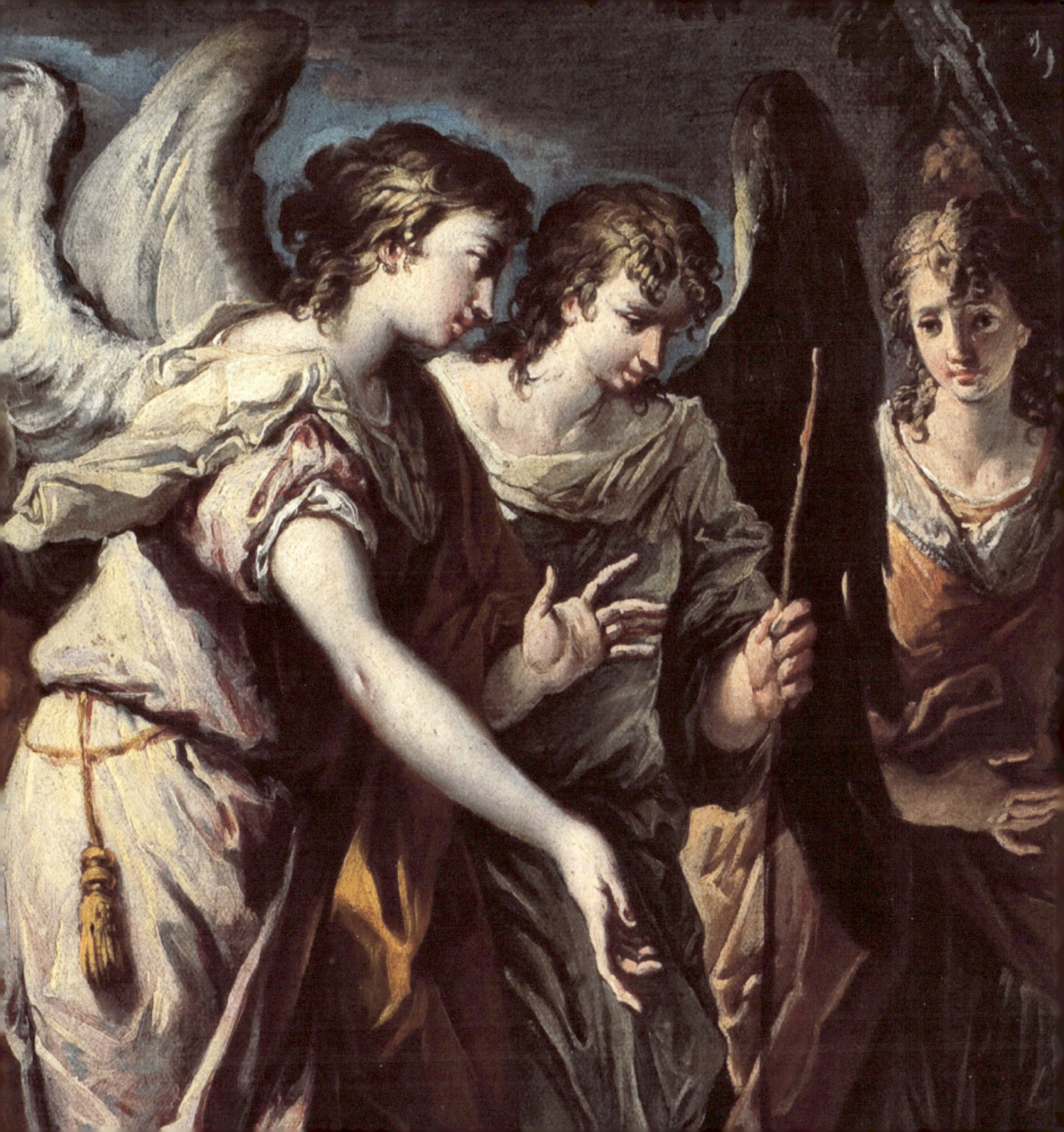

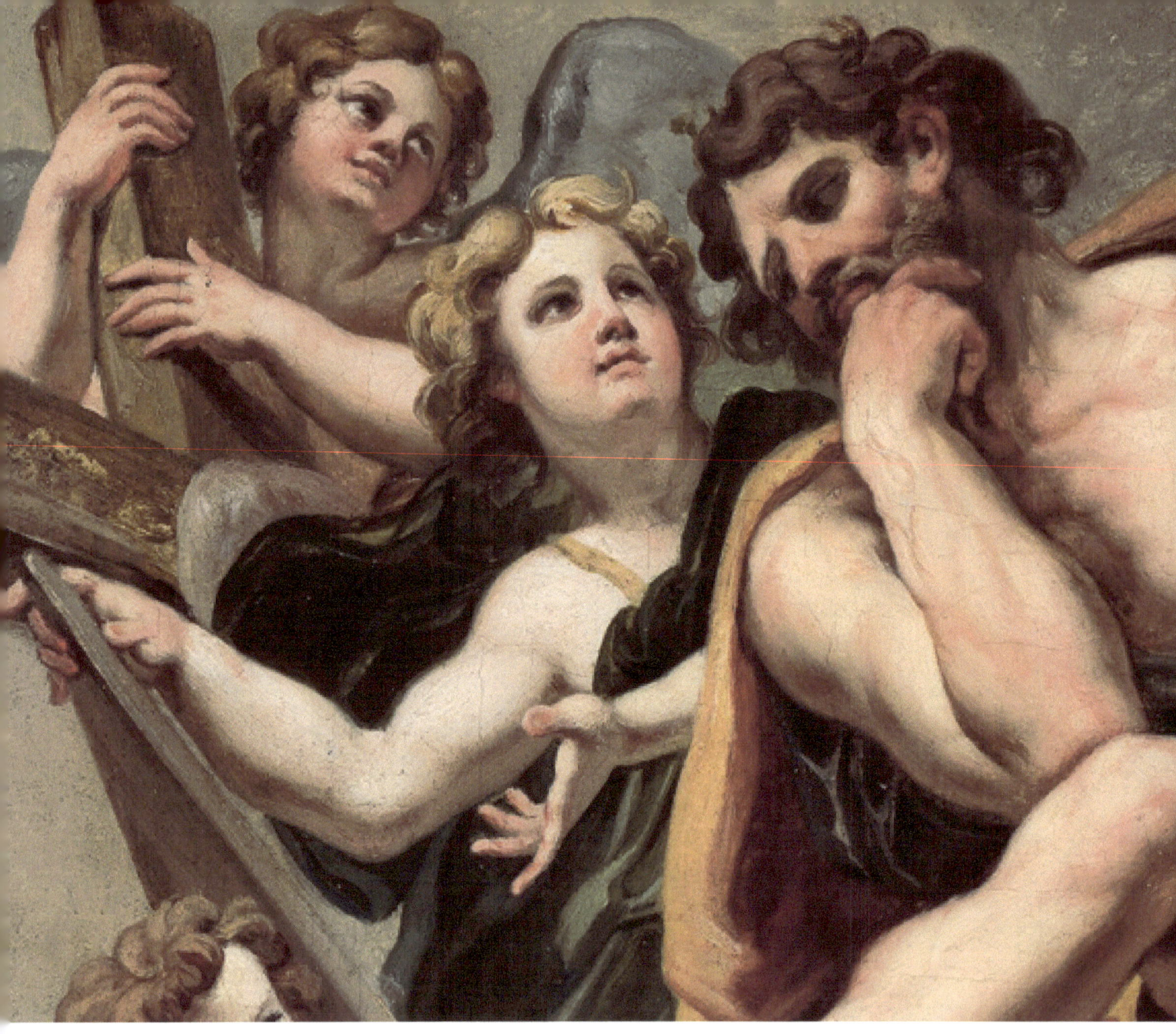

Saint Matthew and Angels (1863)
Rafał Hadziewicz (Polish, 1803-1886)

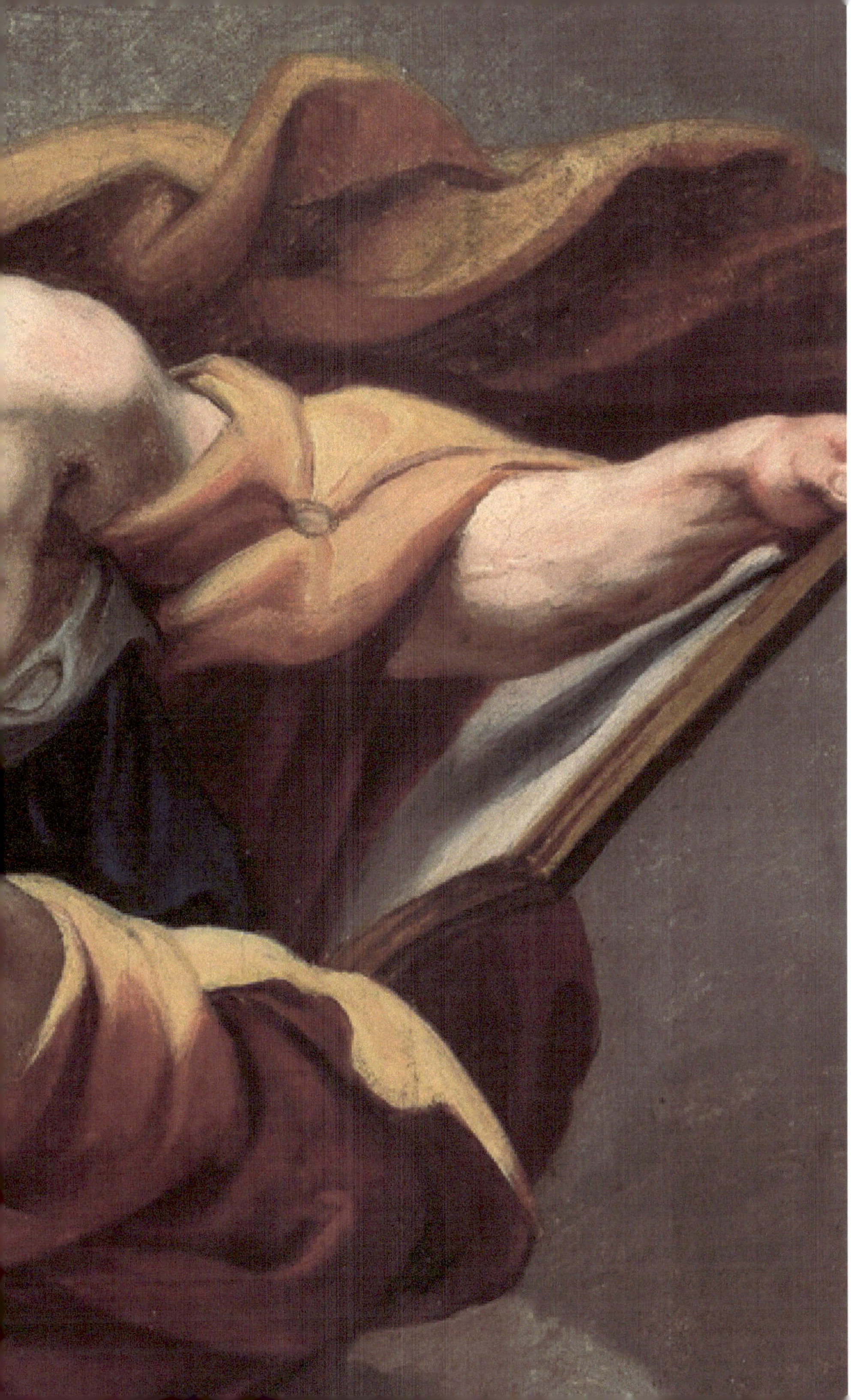

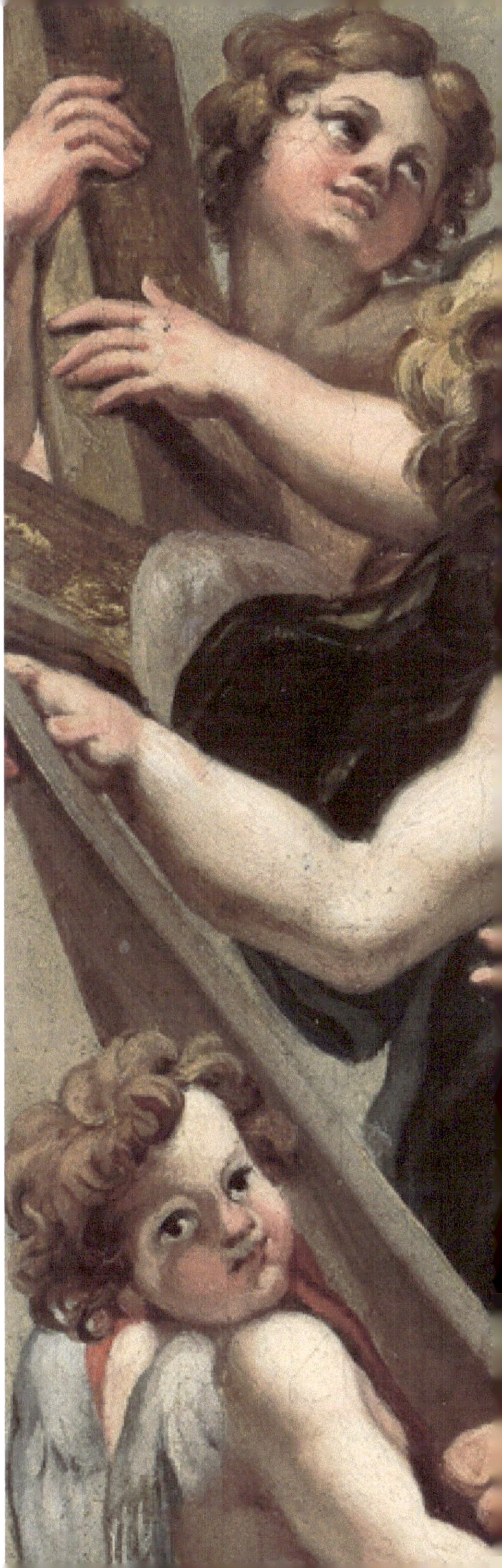

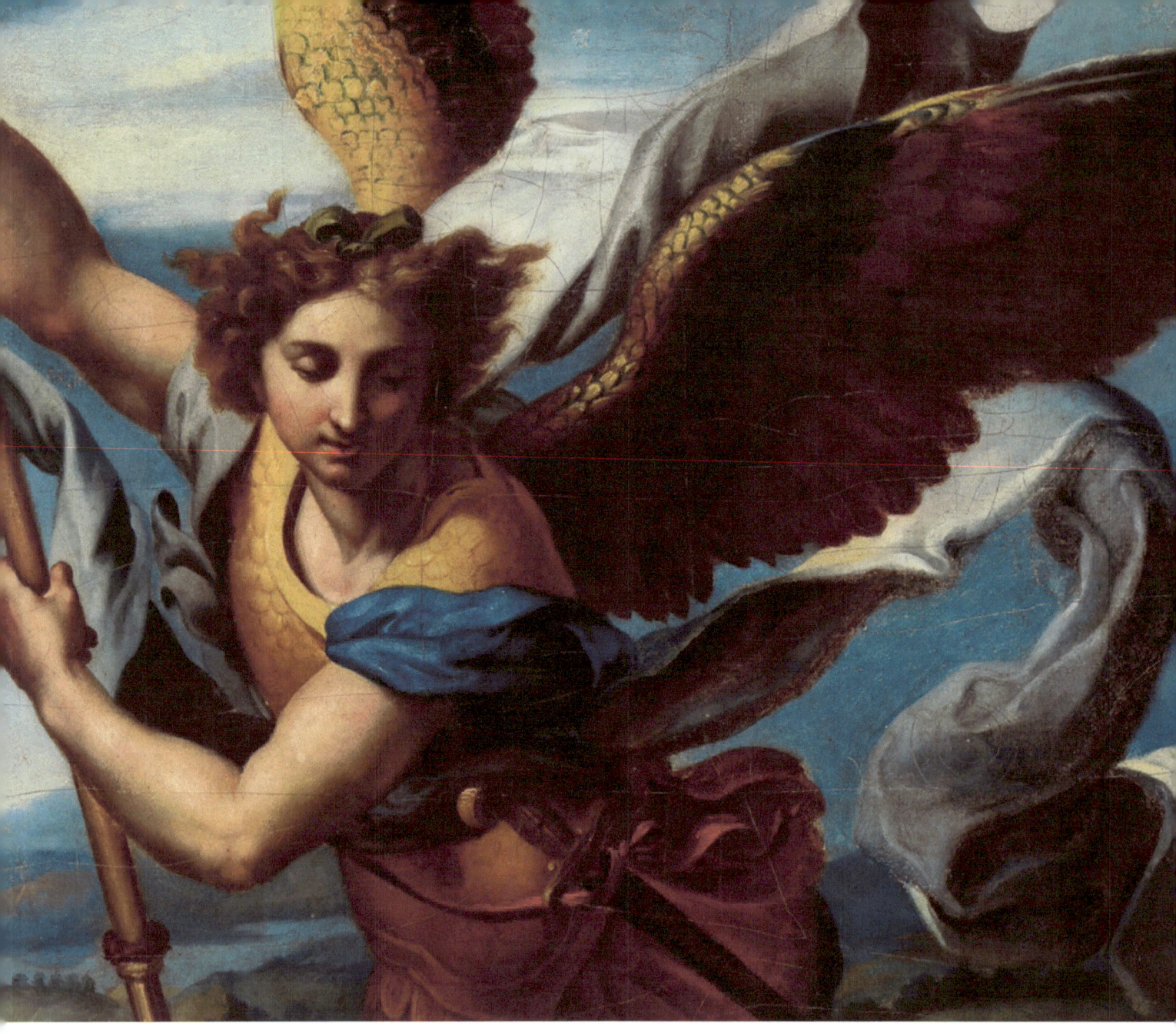

Saint Michael the Archangel Vanquishing Satan (1830)
Rafał Hadziewicz (Polish, 1803-1886)

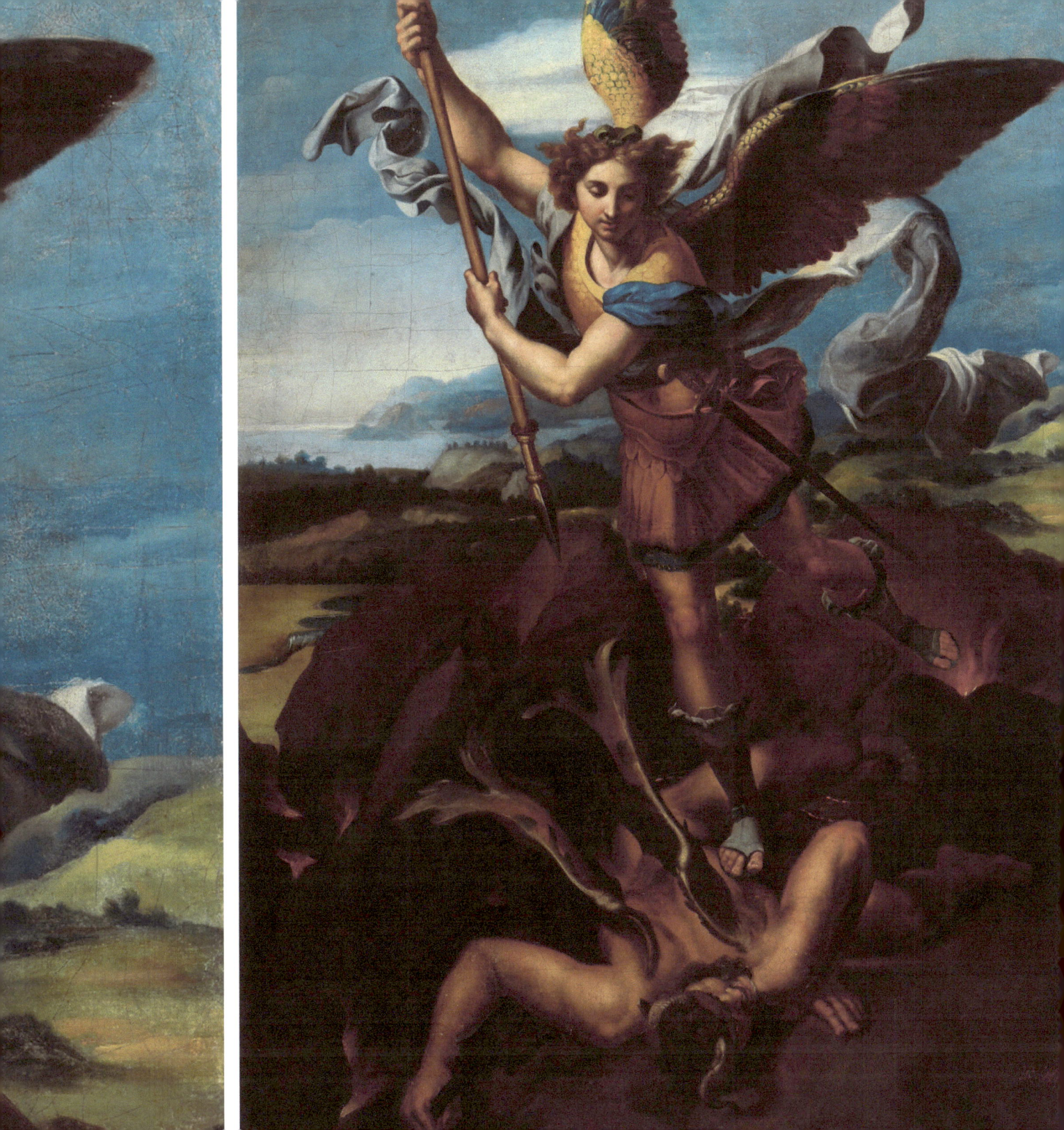

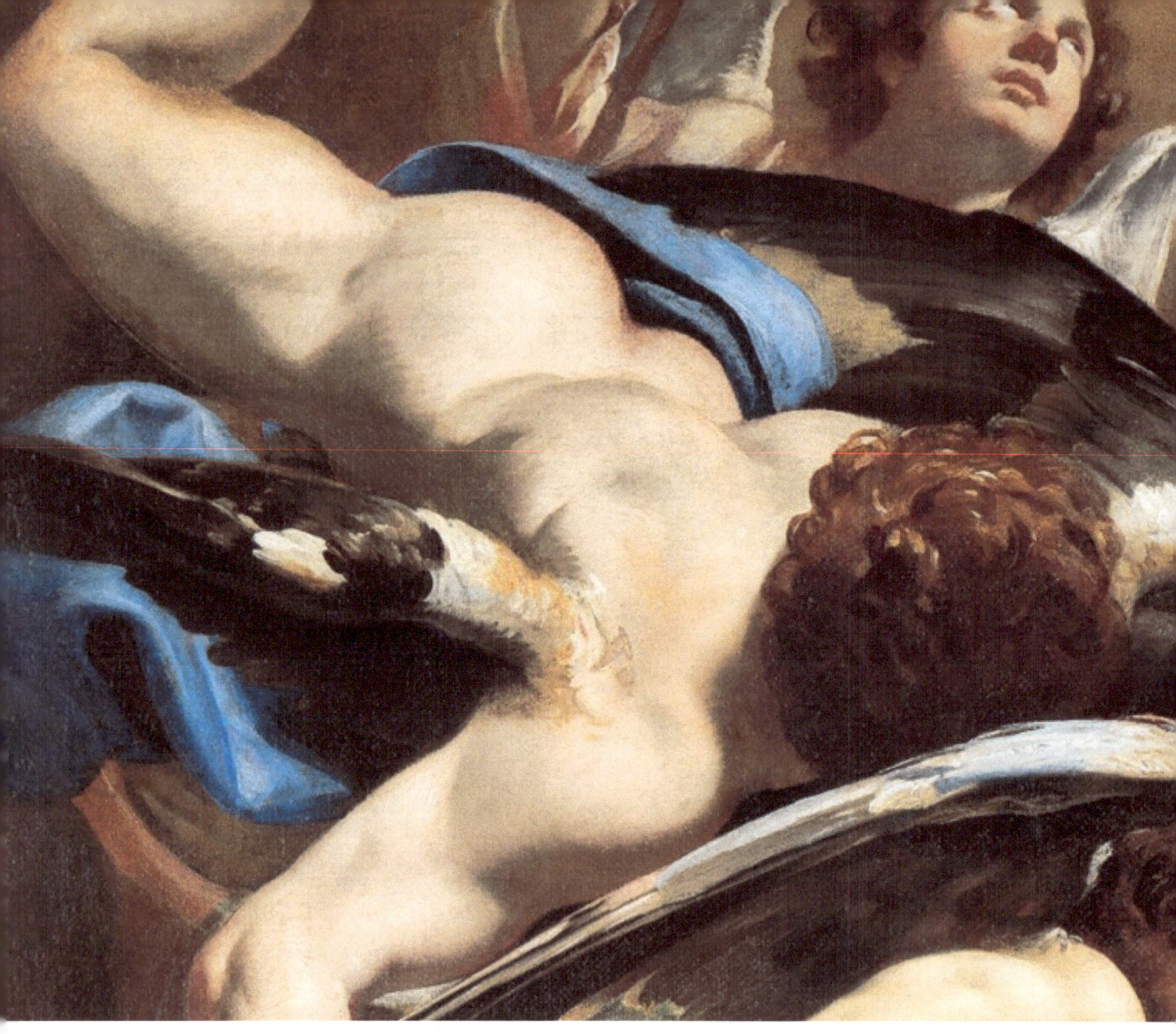

Angels Bearing the Column of the Passion
Simon Vouet (French, 1590-1649)

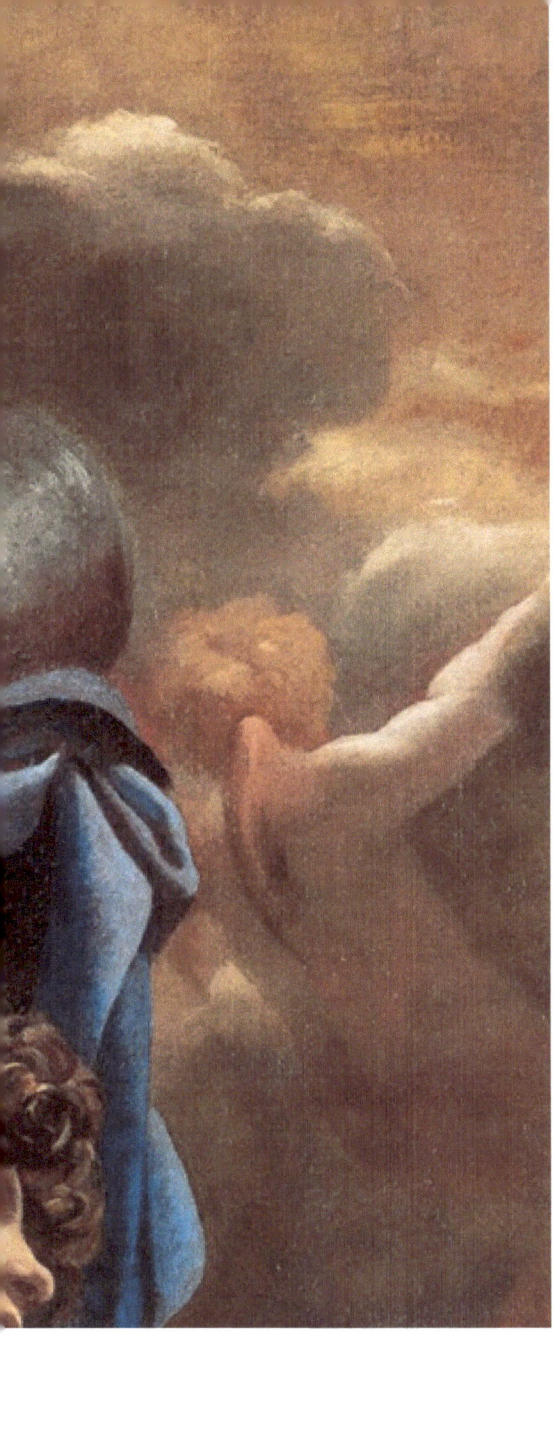

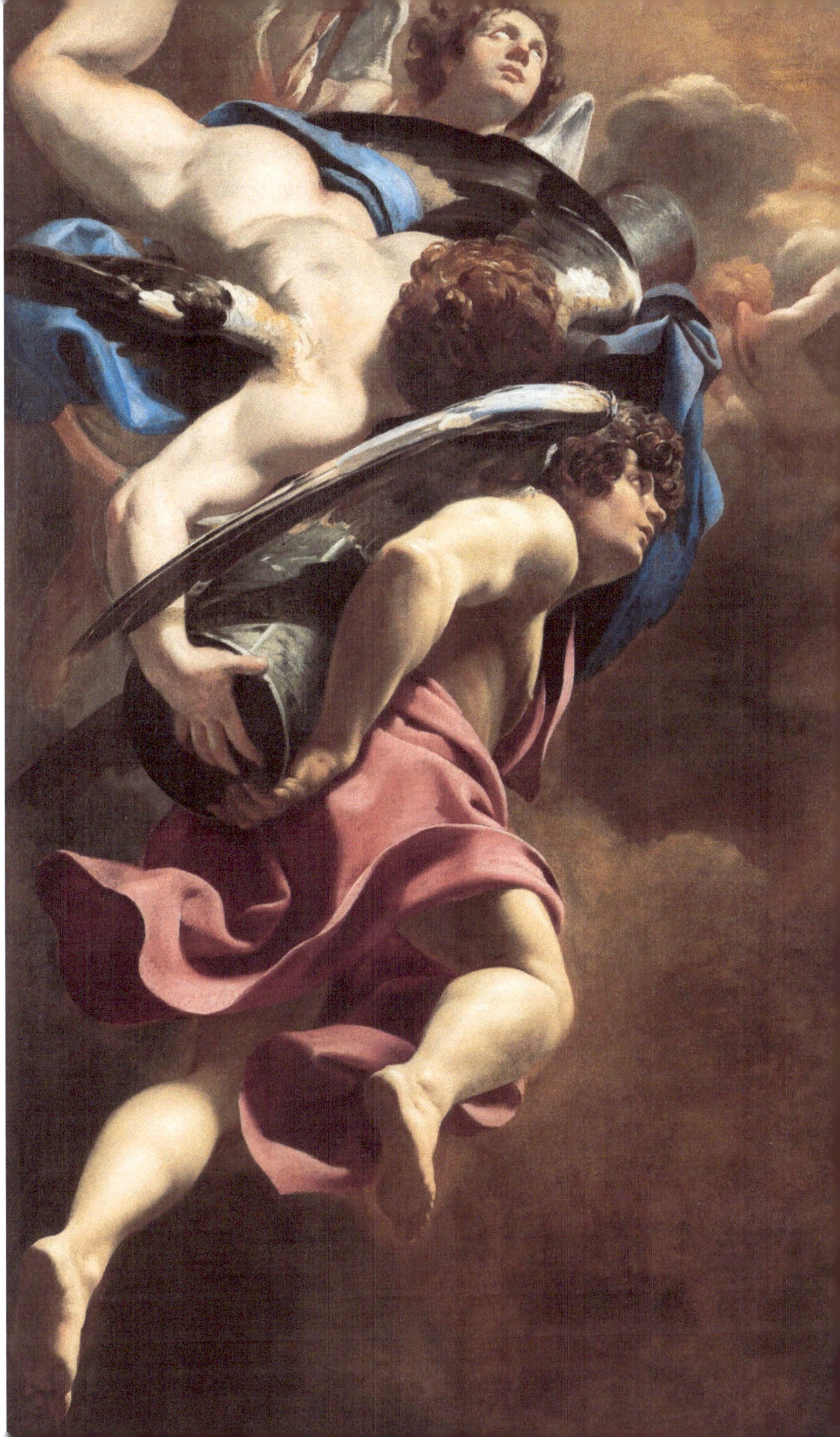

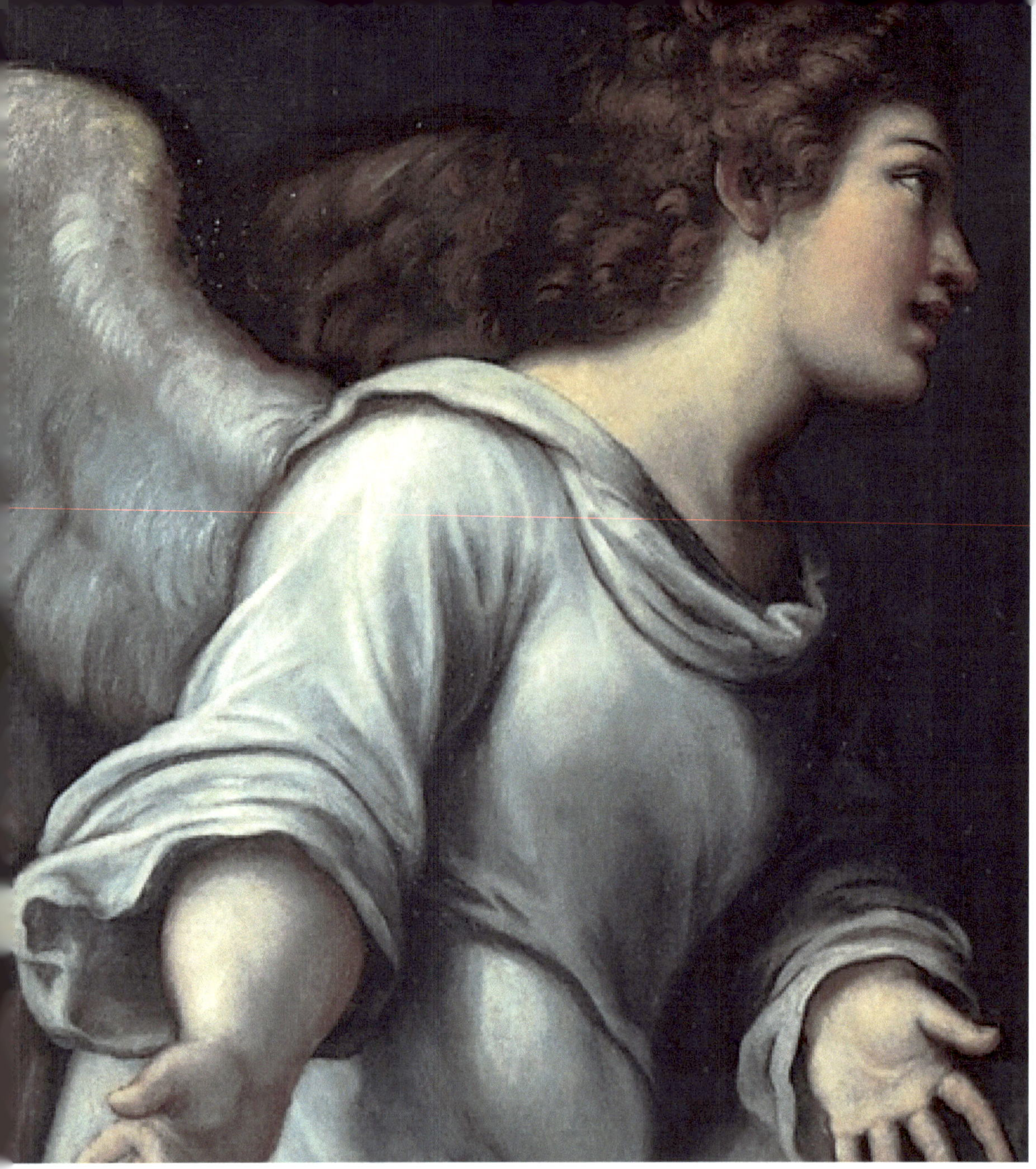

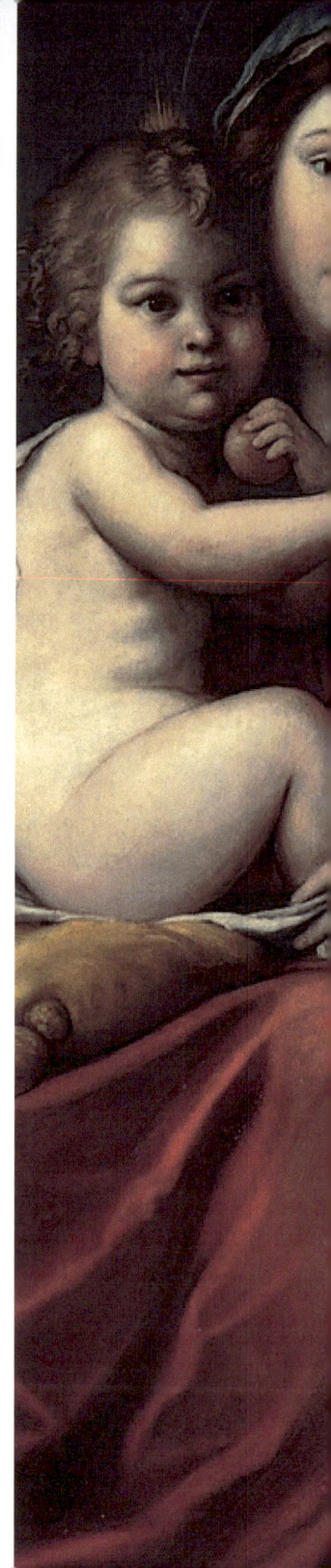

Madonna with the Child and angels (1610 - 1615)
Francesco Albani (Italian, 1578 - 1660)

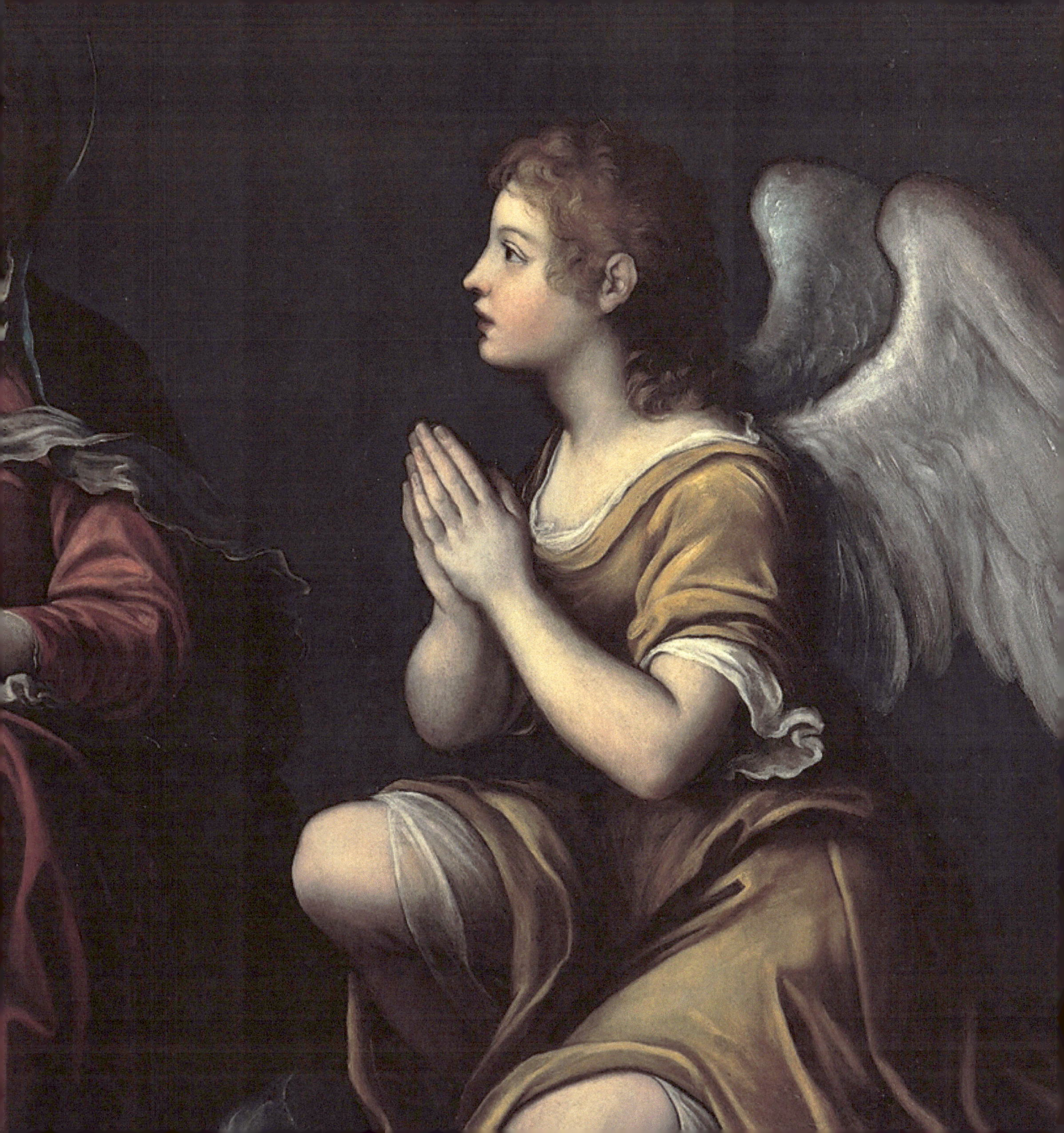

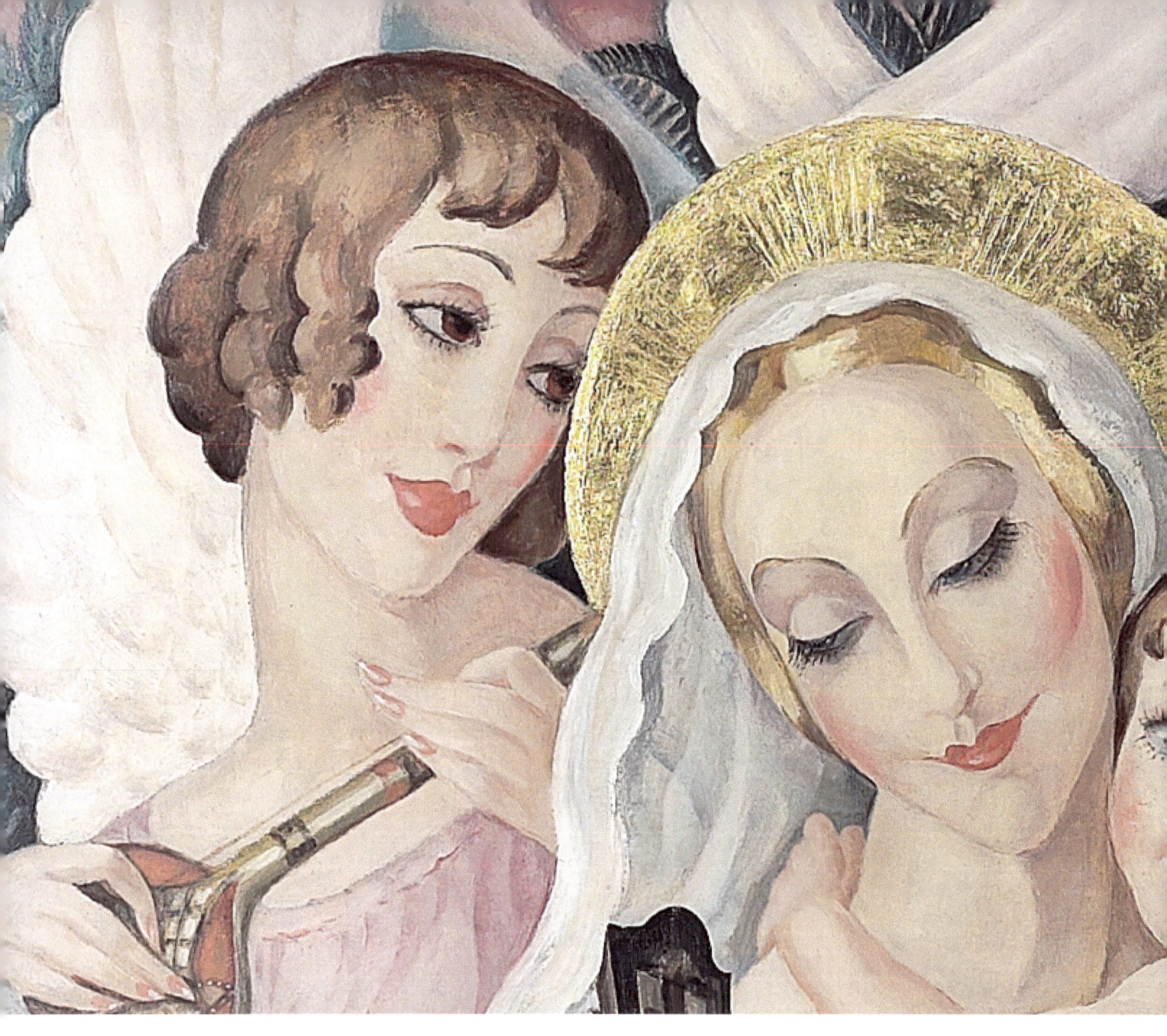

Madonna with child, surrounded by musical angels (1935)
Gerda Wegener (Danish, 1886 – 1940)

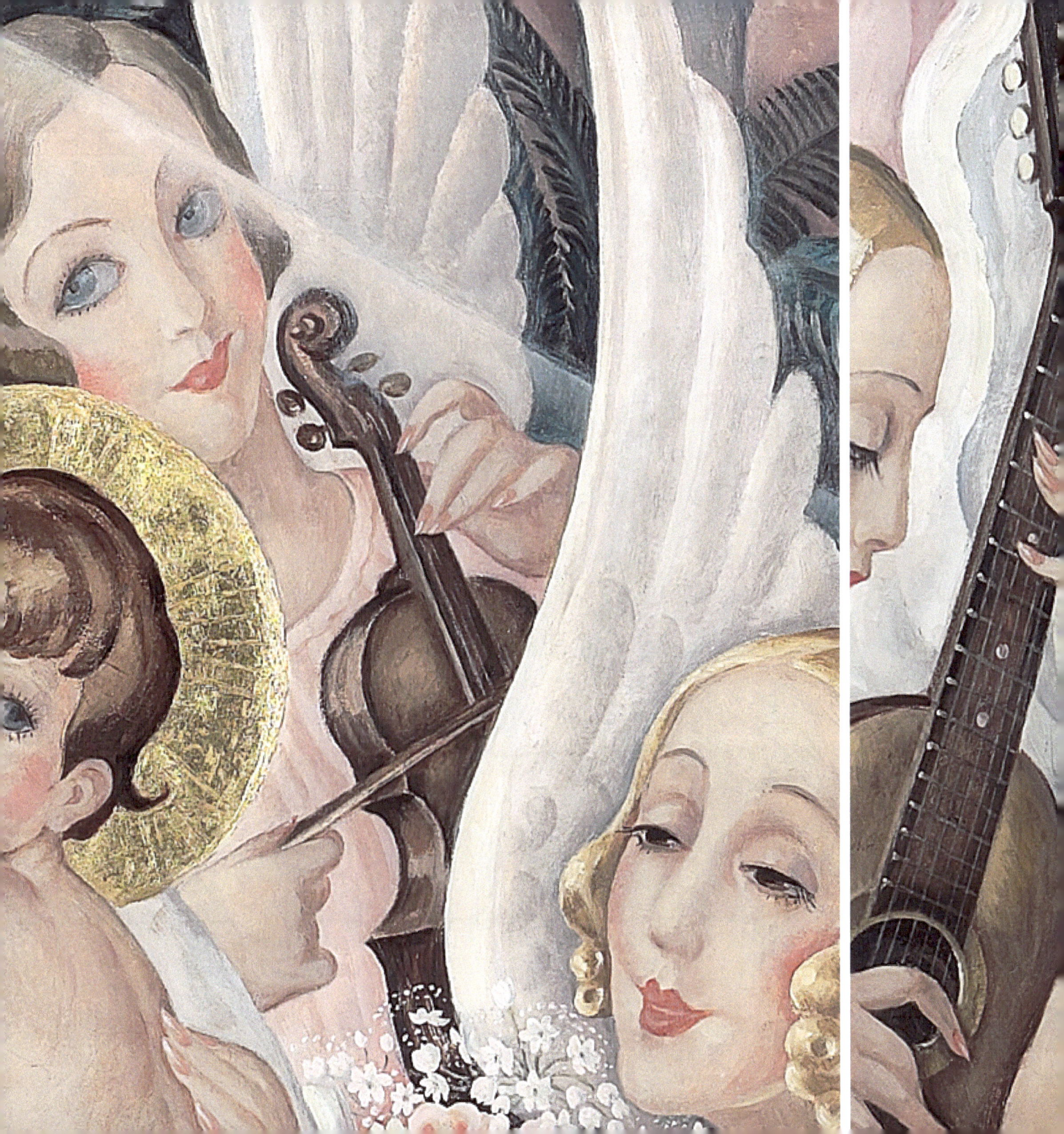

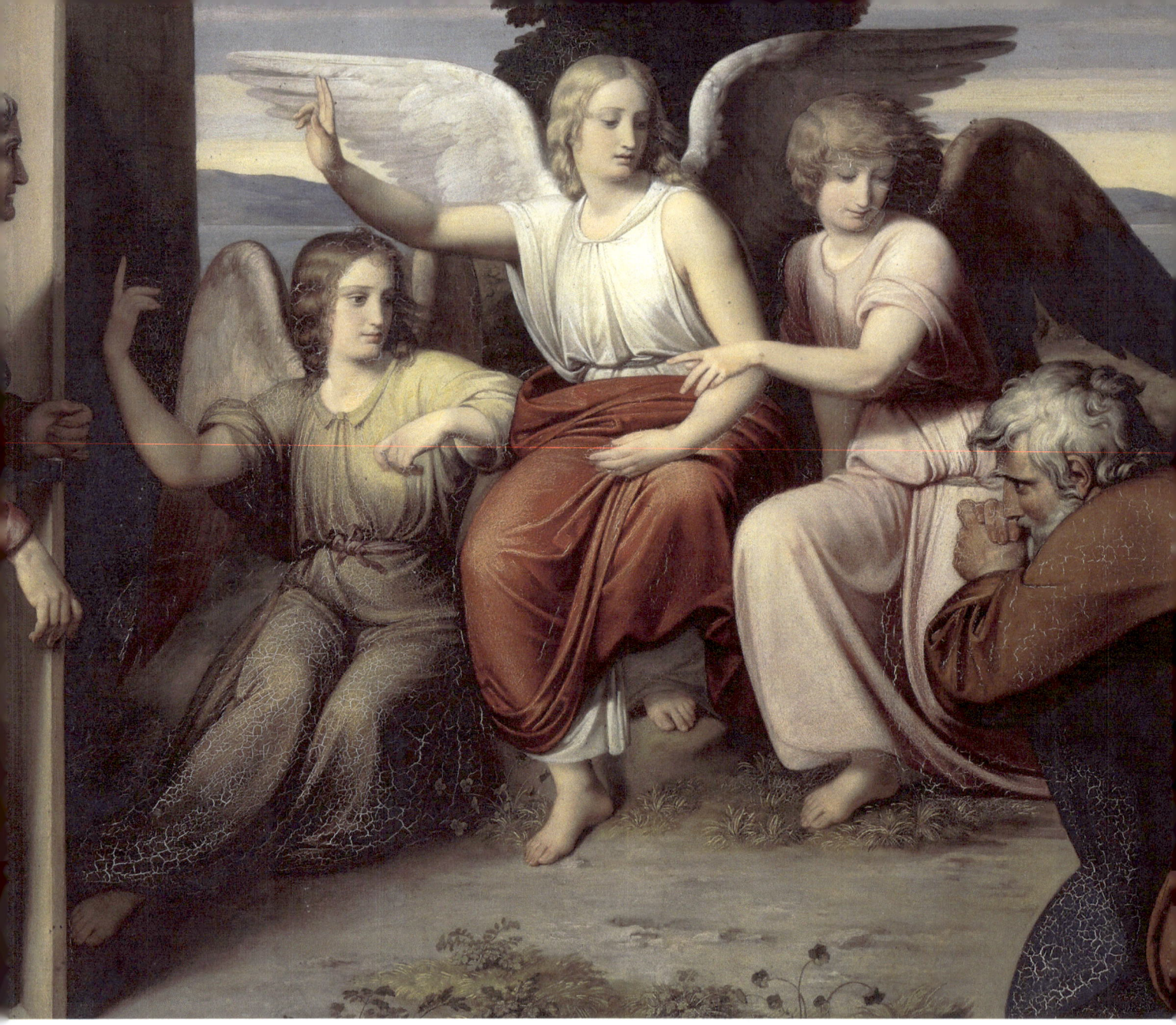

The Angels With Abraham (1830-1832)
Bernhard von Neher the younger (German, 1806-1886)

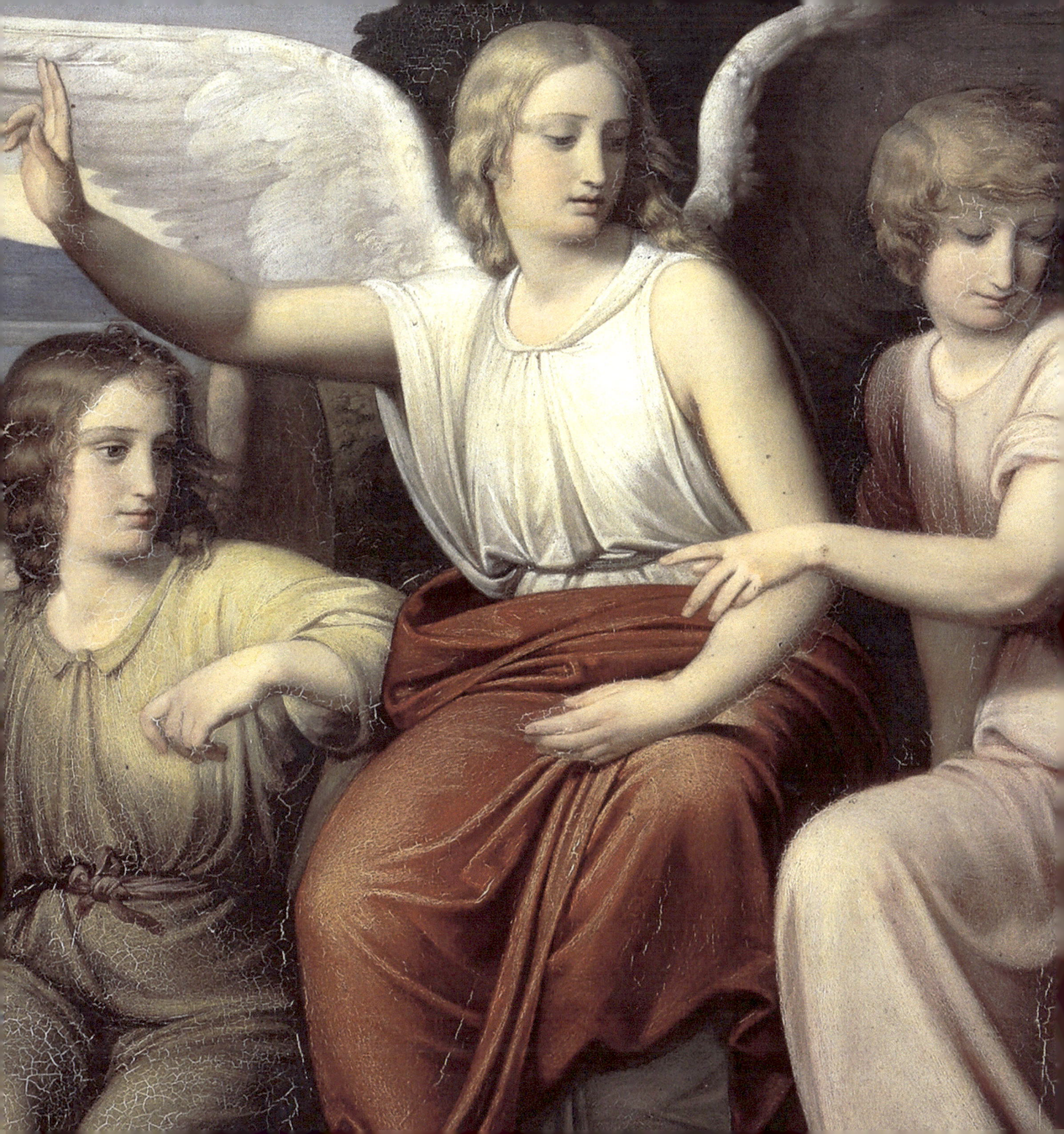

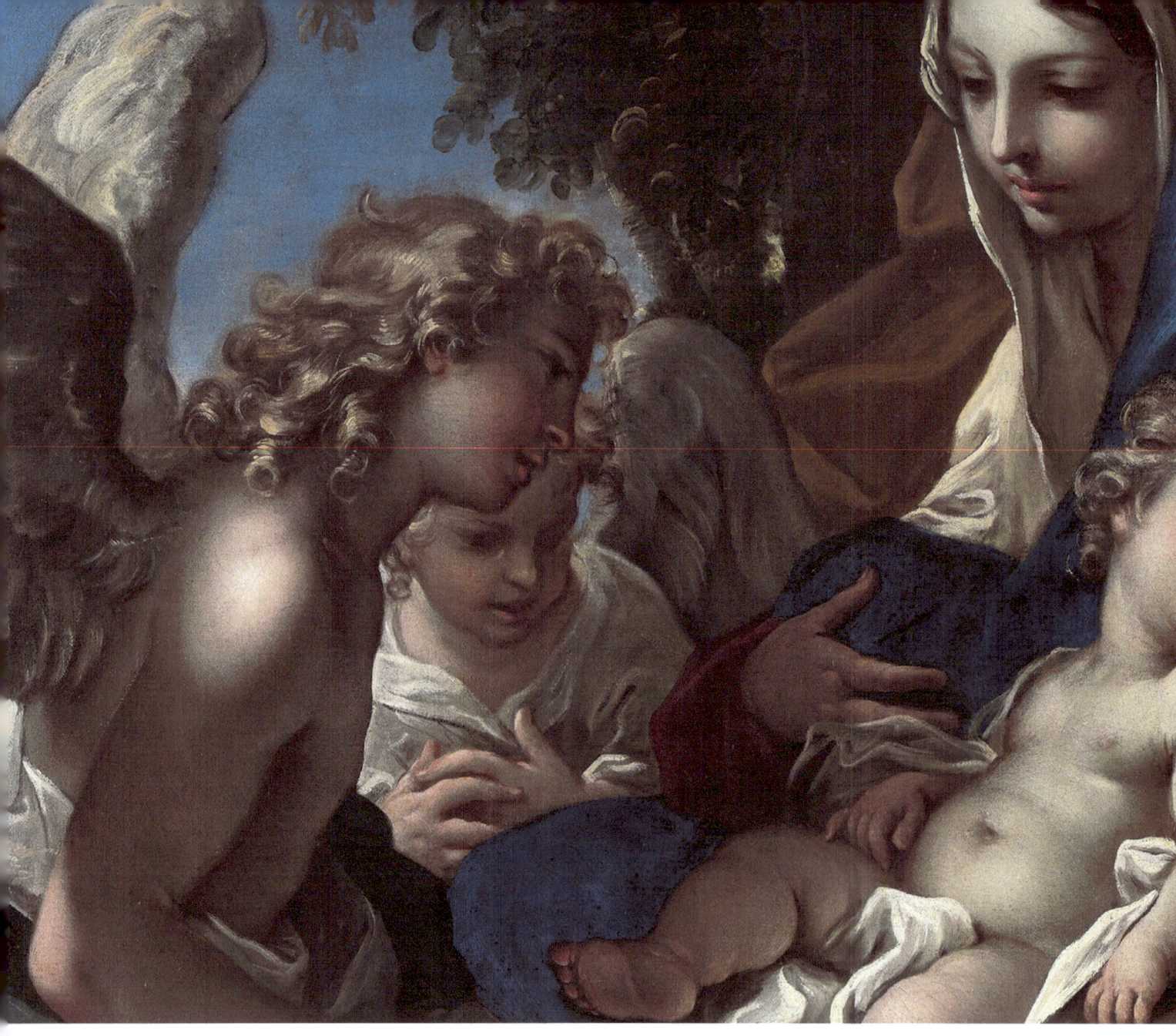

The Holy Family with Angels (ca. 1700)
Sebastiano Ricci (Italian, 1659-1734)

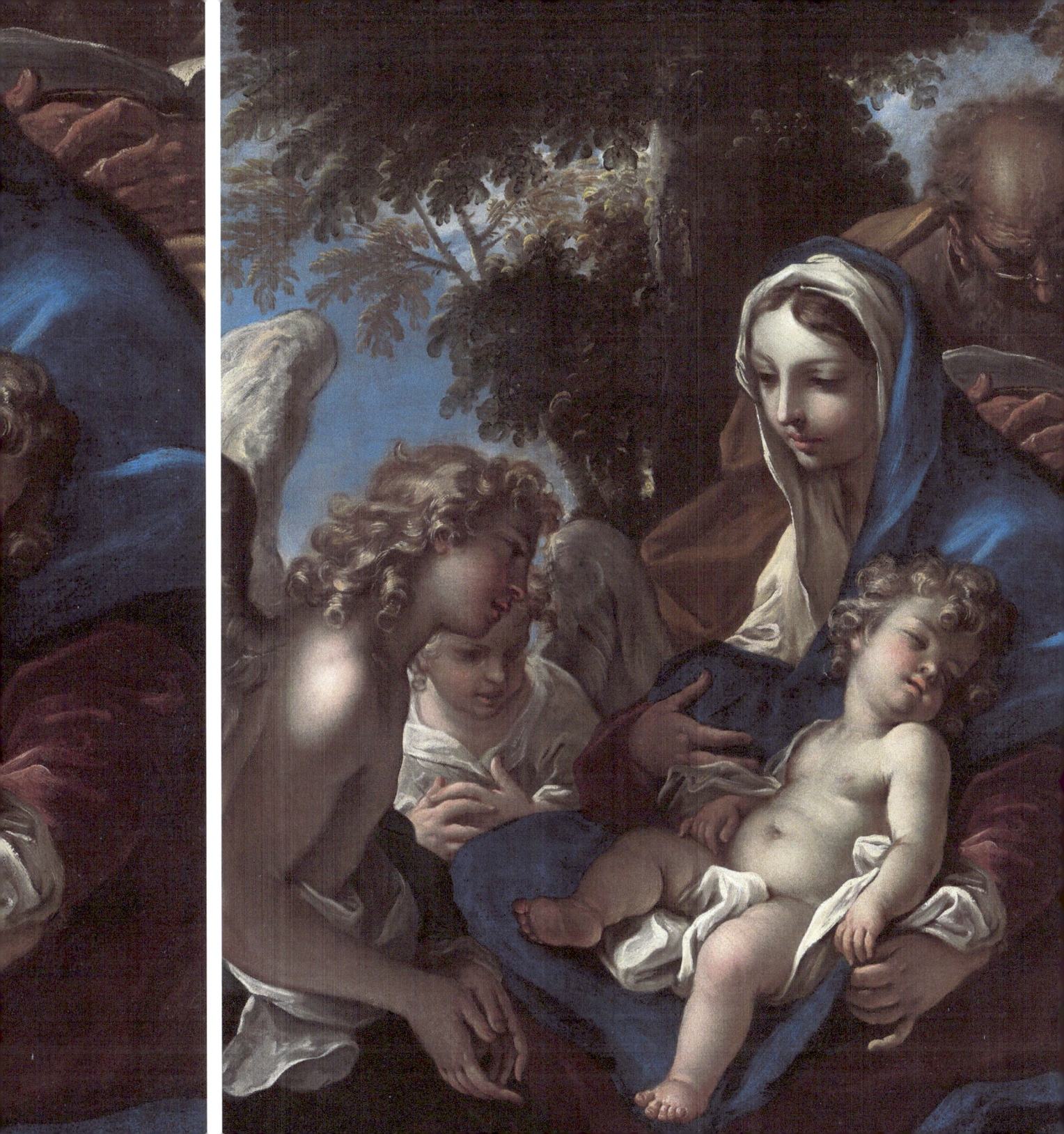

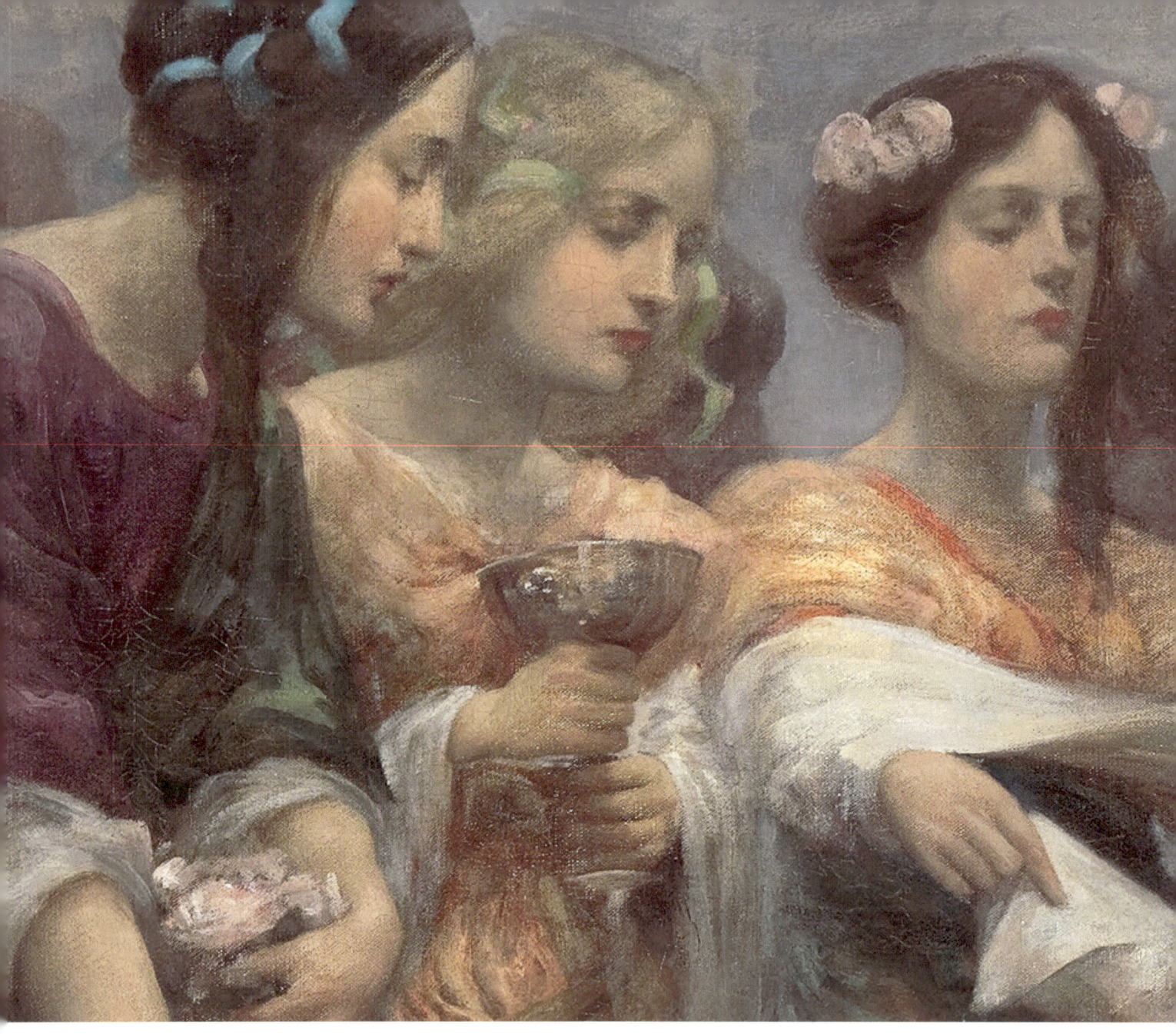

Angels Descending (circa 1897)
Rupert Bunny (Australian, 1864 – 1947)

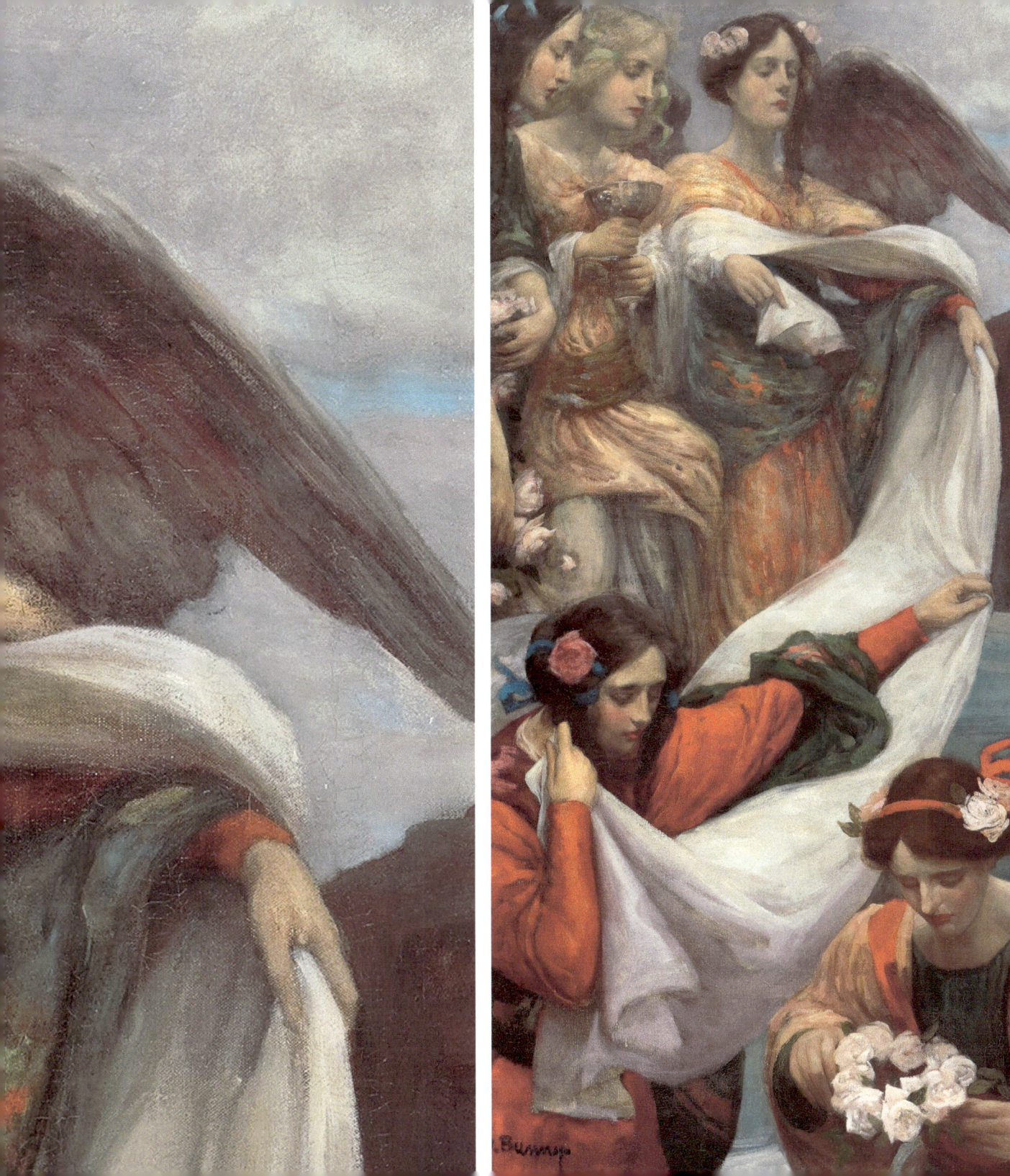

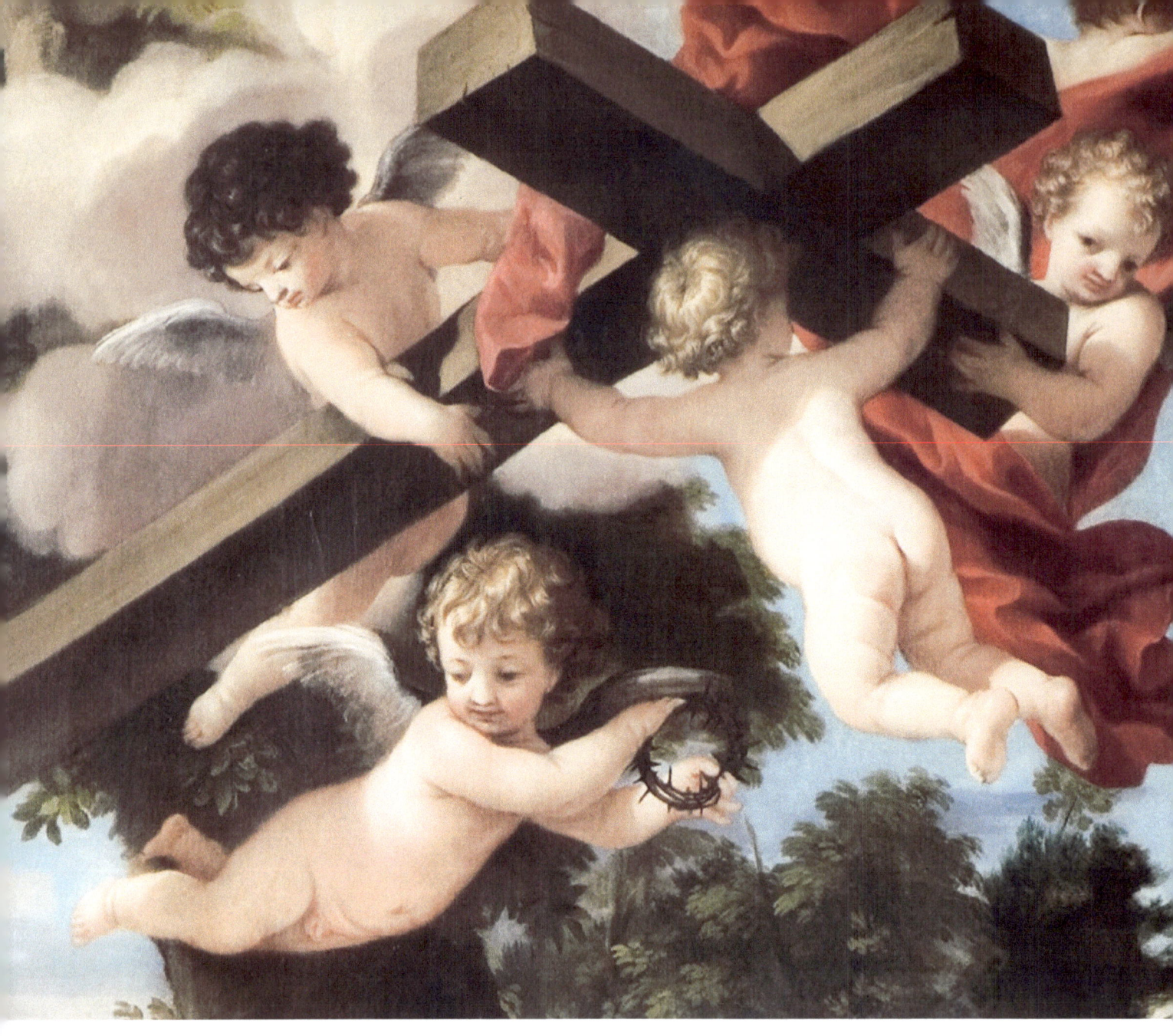

The Holy Family With Angels (1700)
Pietro da Cortona (Italian, 1596-1669)

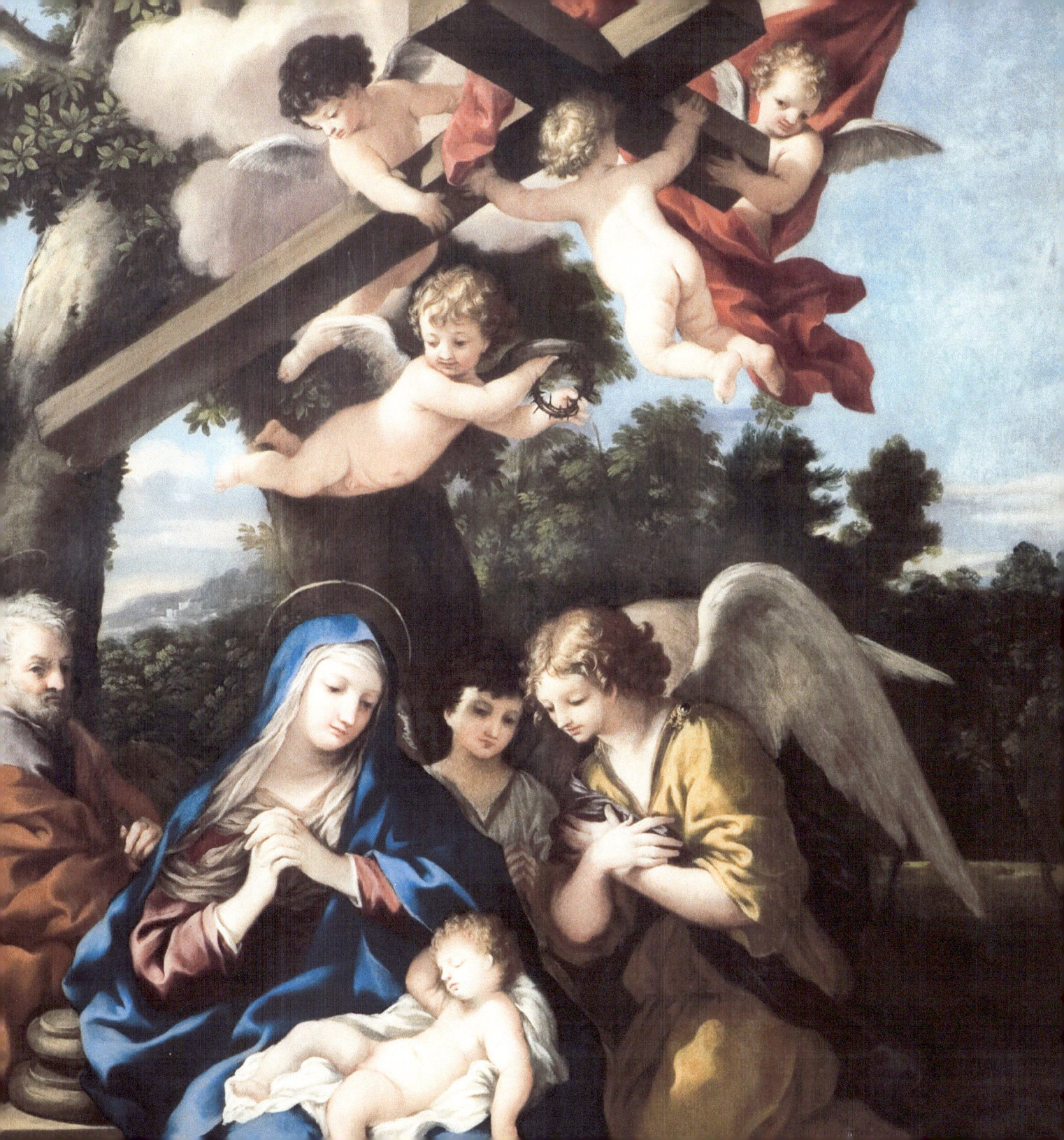

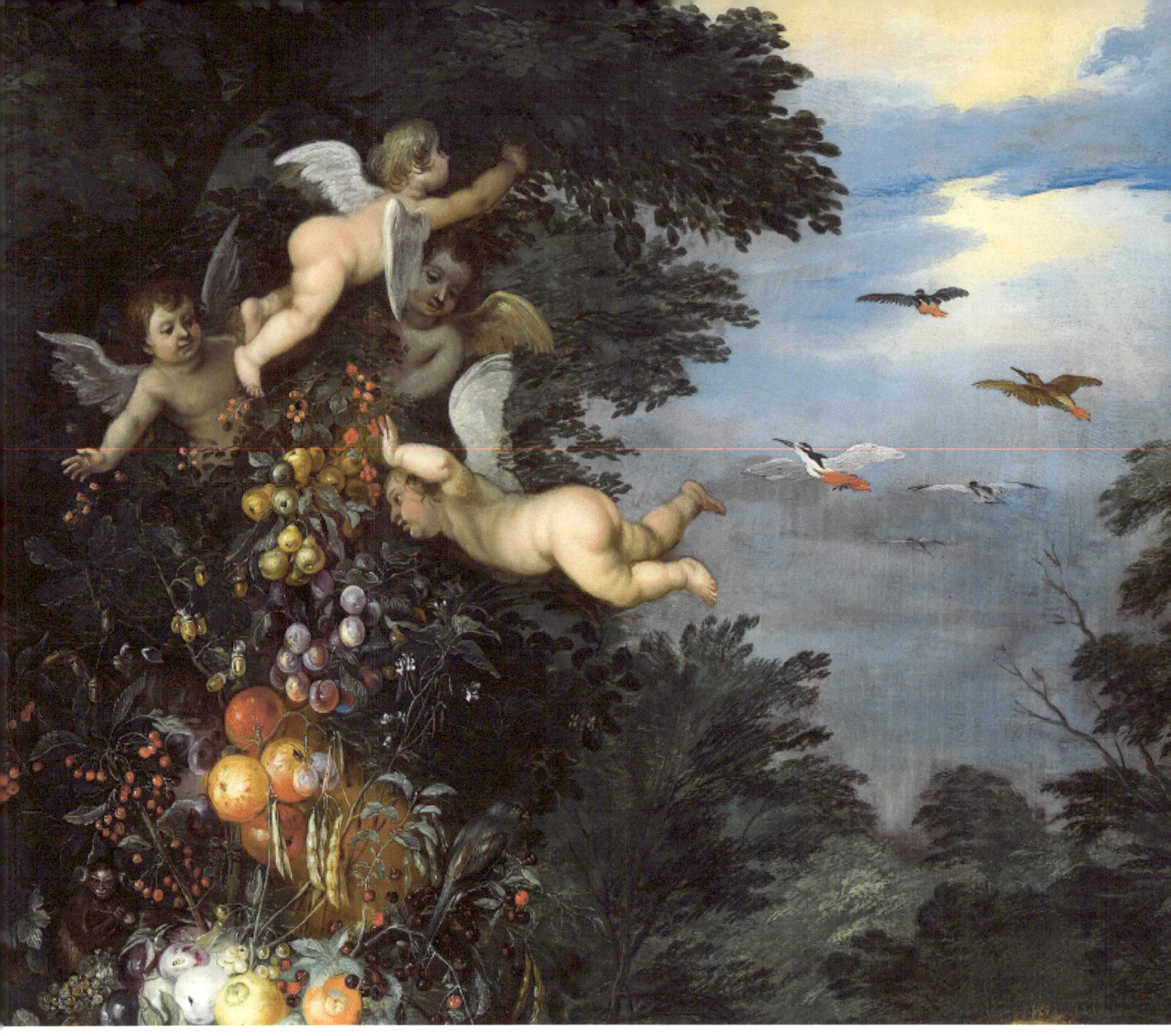

The Holy Family Within A Garland Of Fruit, Flowers And Vegetables Held By Angels
Jan Brueghel the Younger (Flemish, 1601 - 1678)

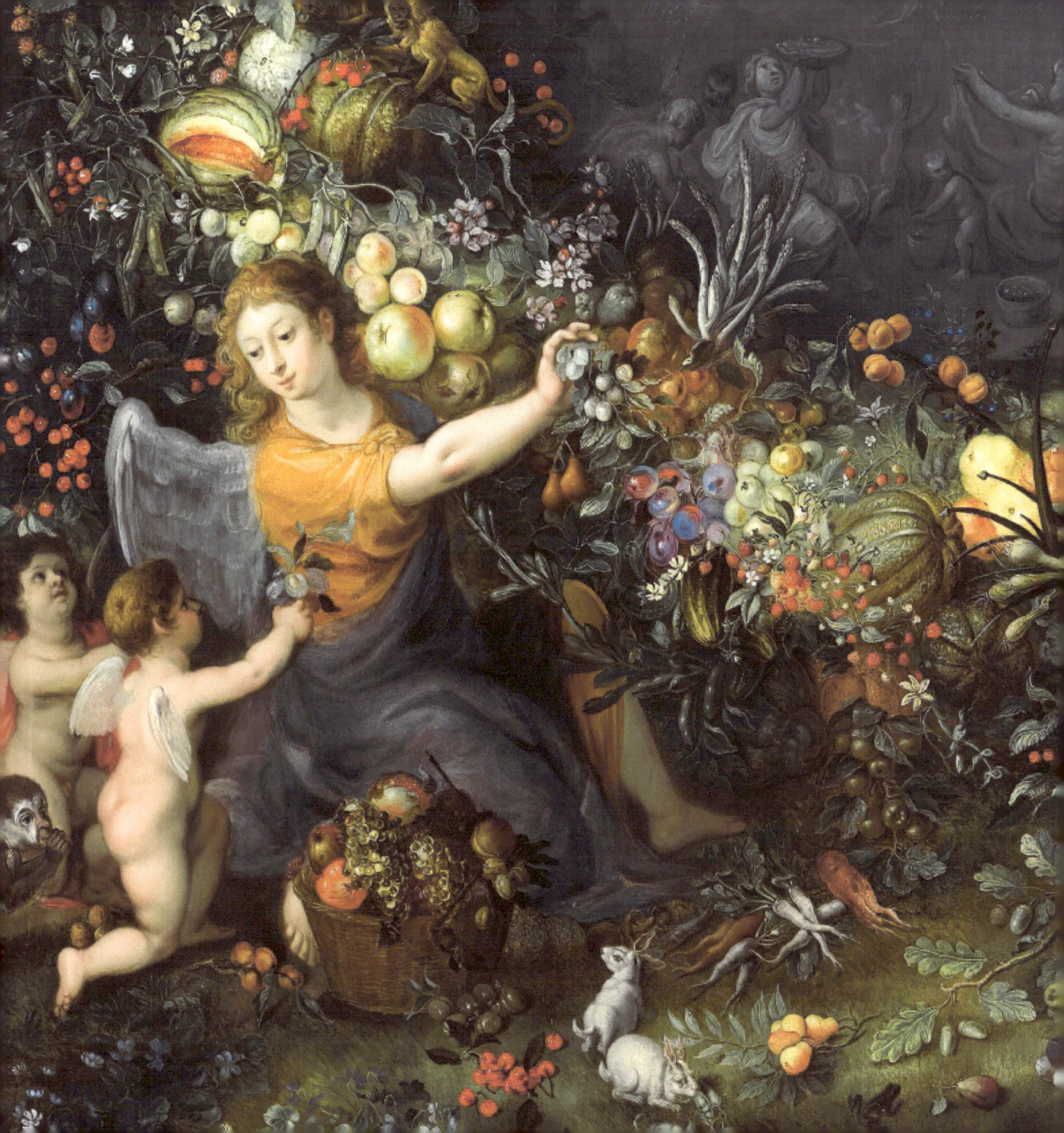

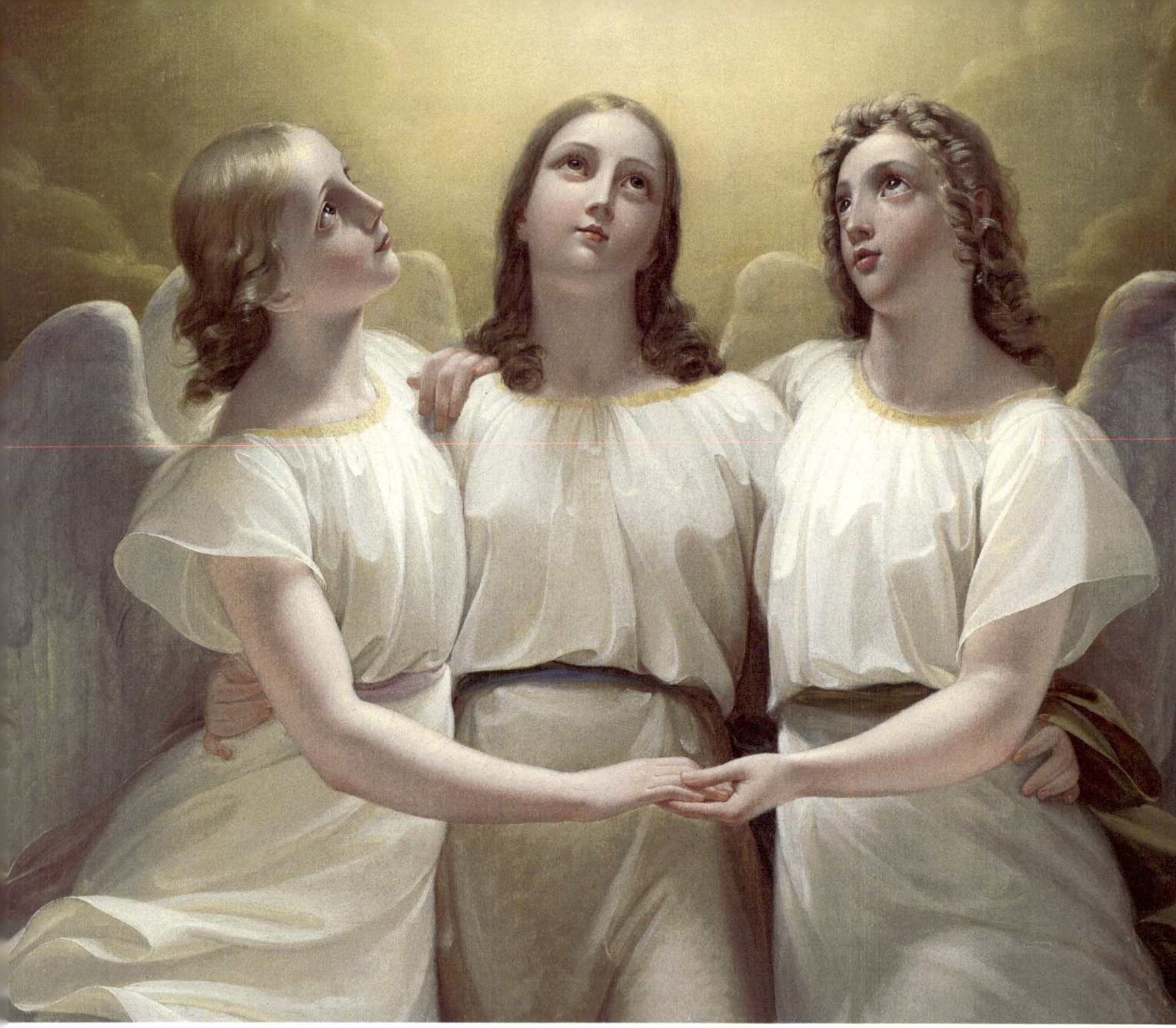

Three Guardian Angels (1822)
Franz Kadlik (Czech, 1786-1840)

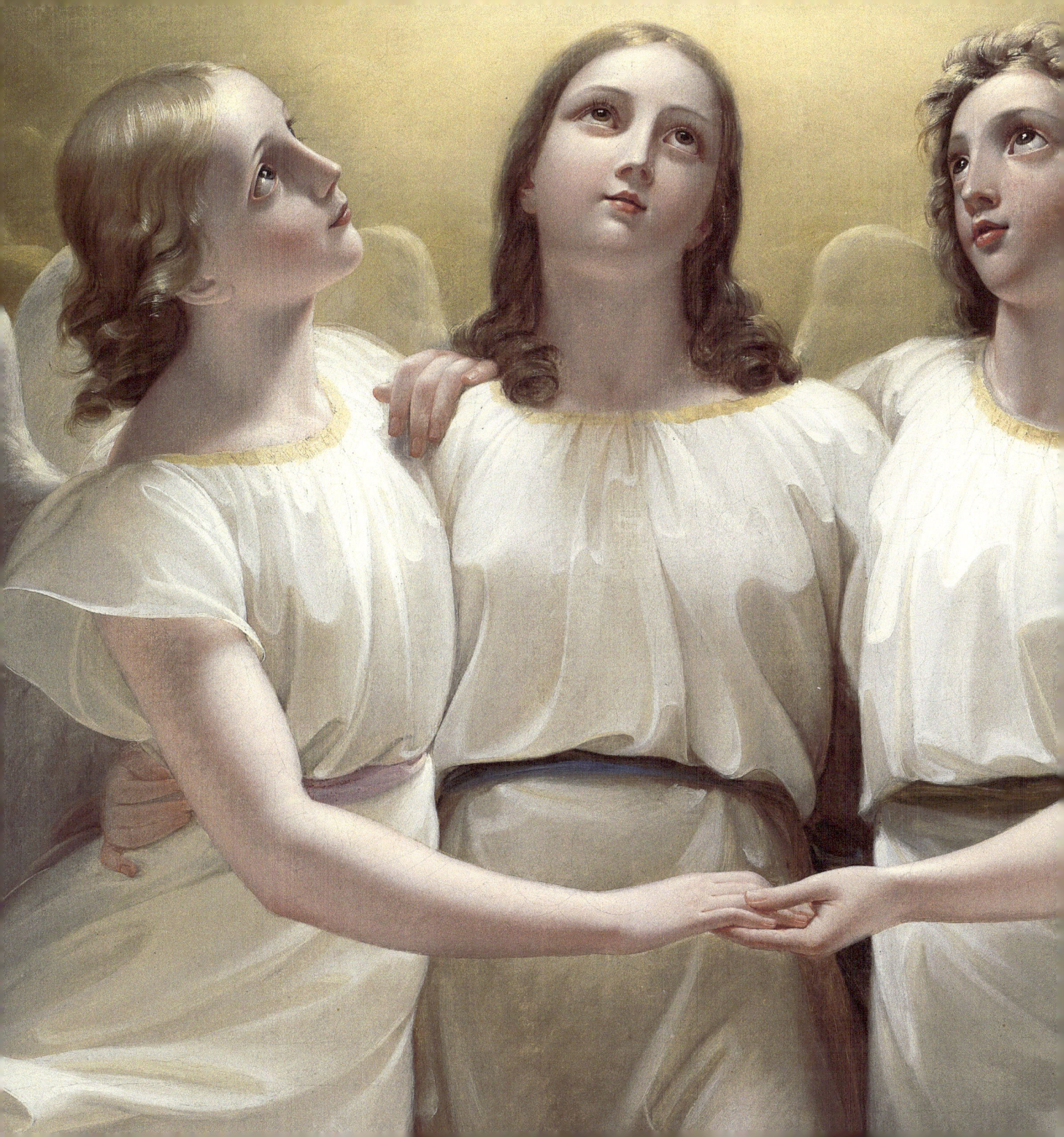

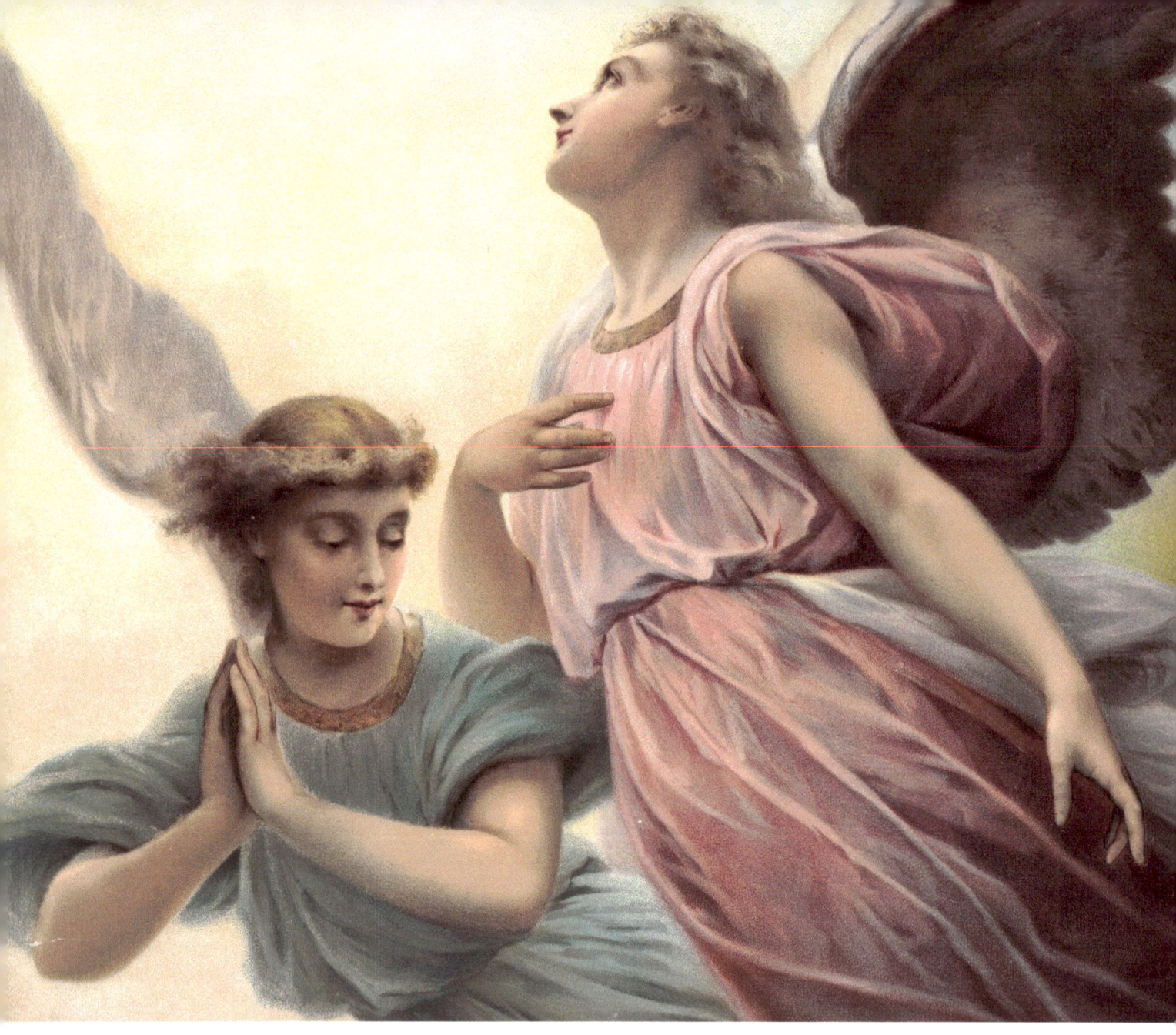

Guardian angels (1892)
Knapp & Co. (American, 19th Century)

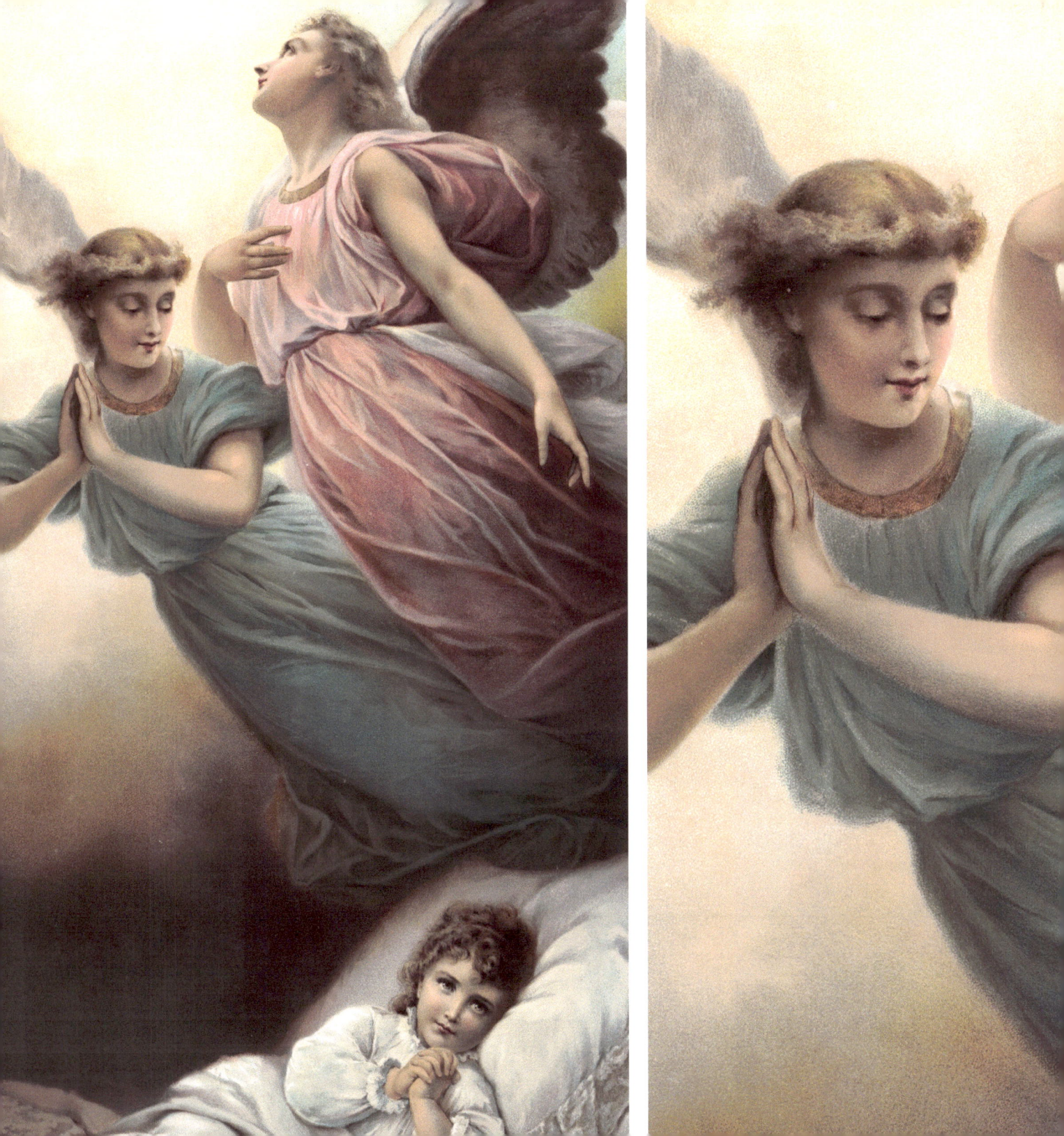

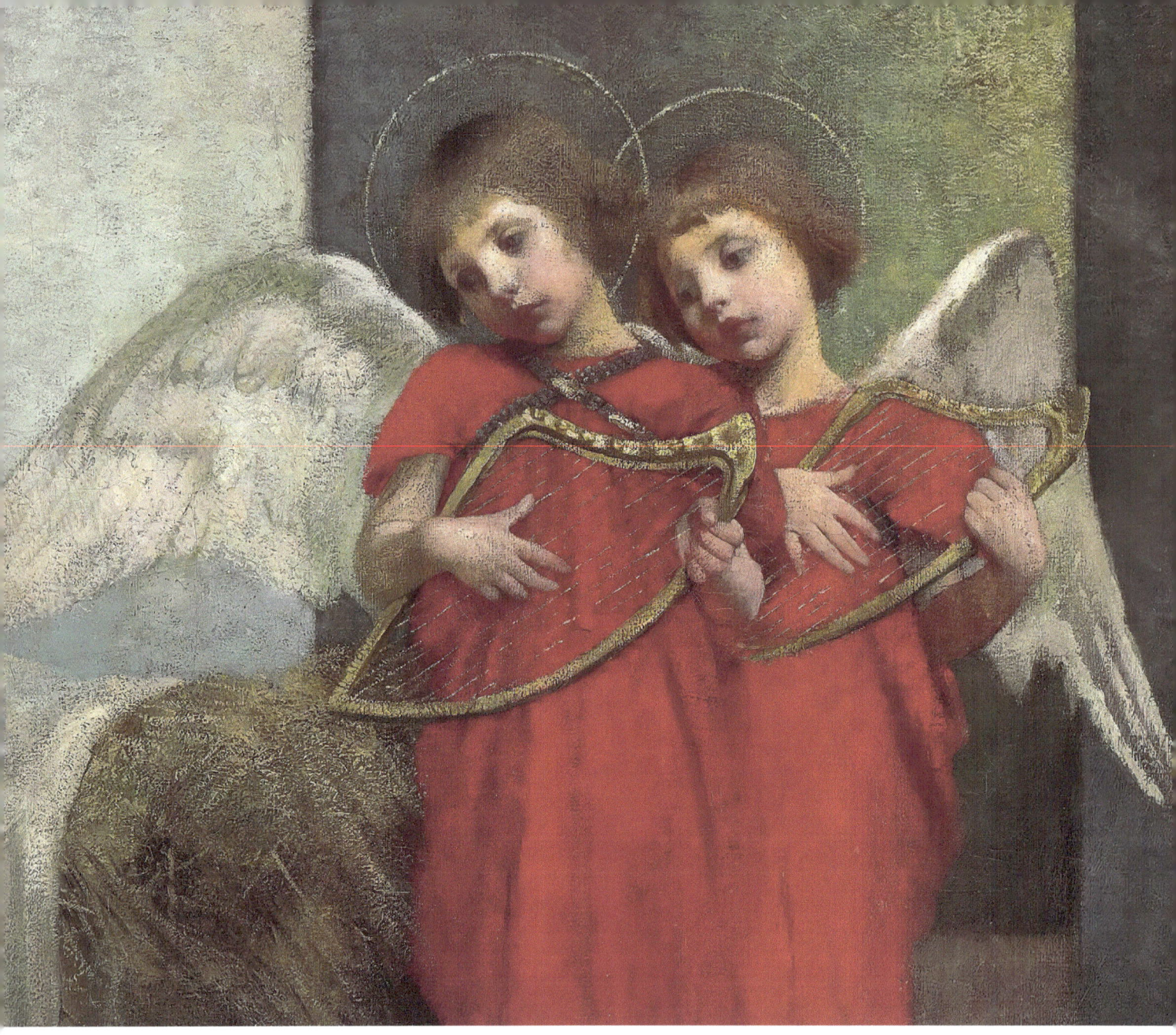

Angels Entertaining the Holy Child
Marianne Stokes (Austrian, 1855–1927)

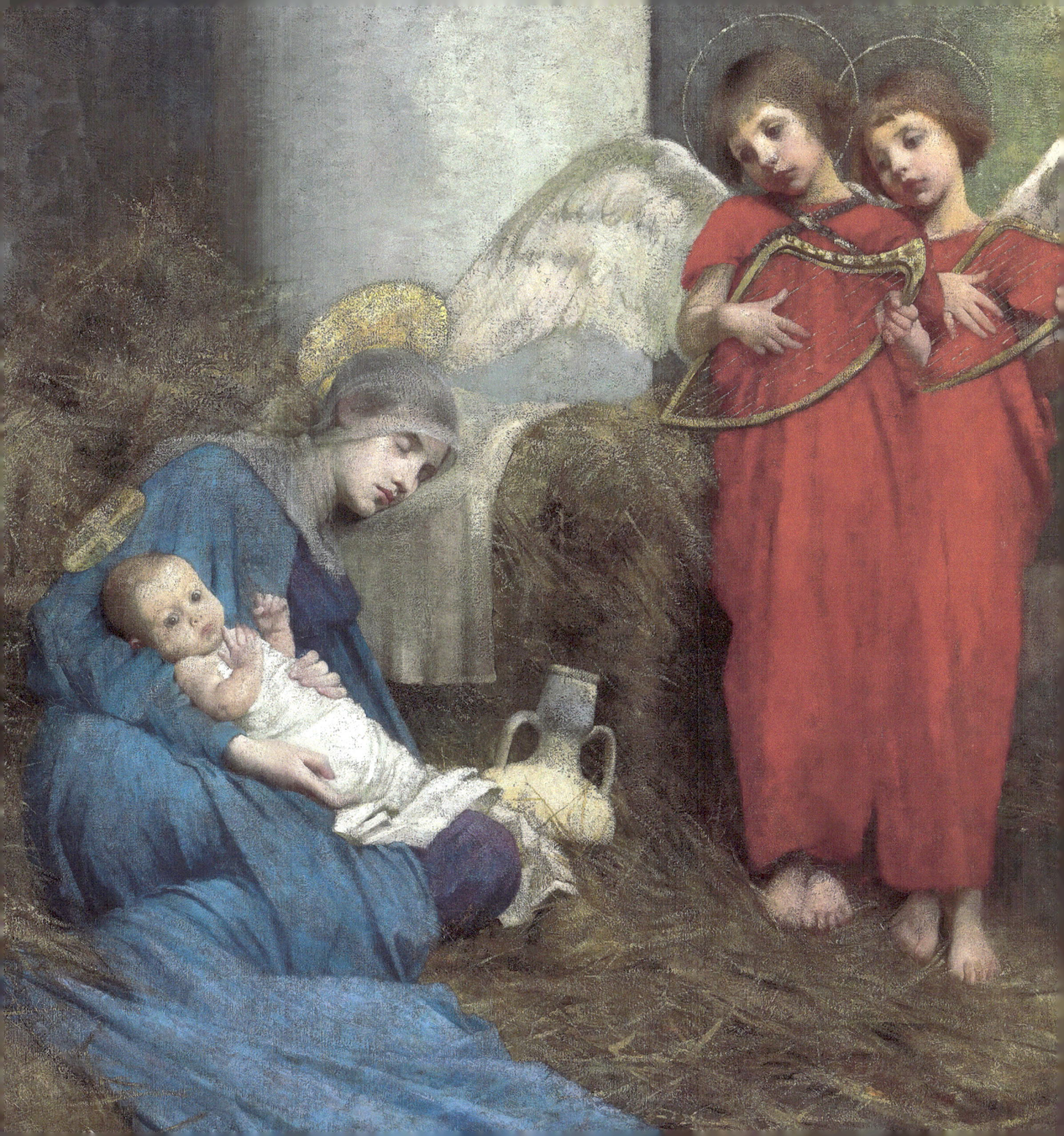

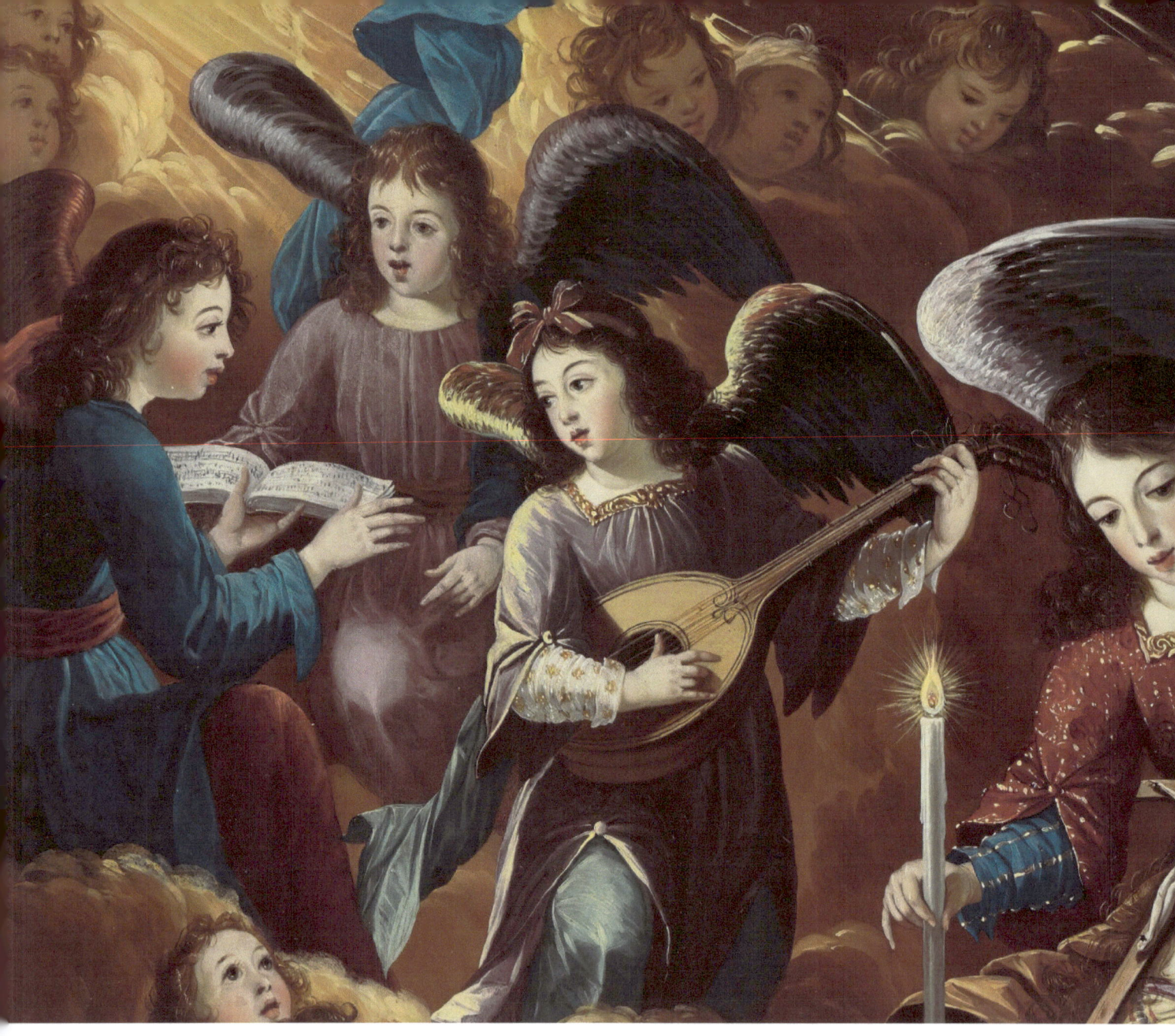

The Penitent Magdalene Comforted By Angels (1679)
Josefa de Ayala e Cabrera (Spanish, 1630 - 1684)

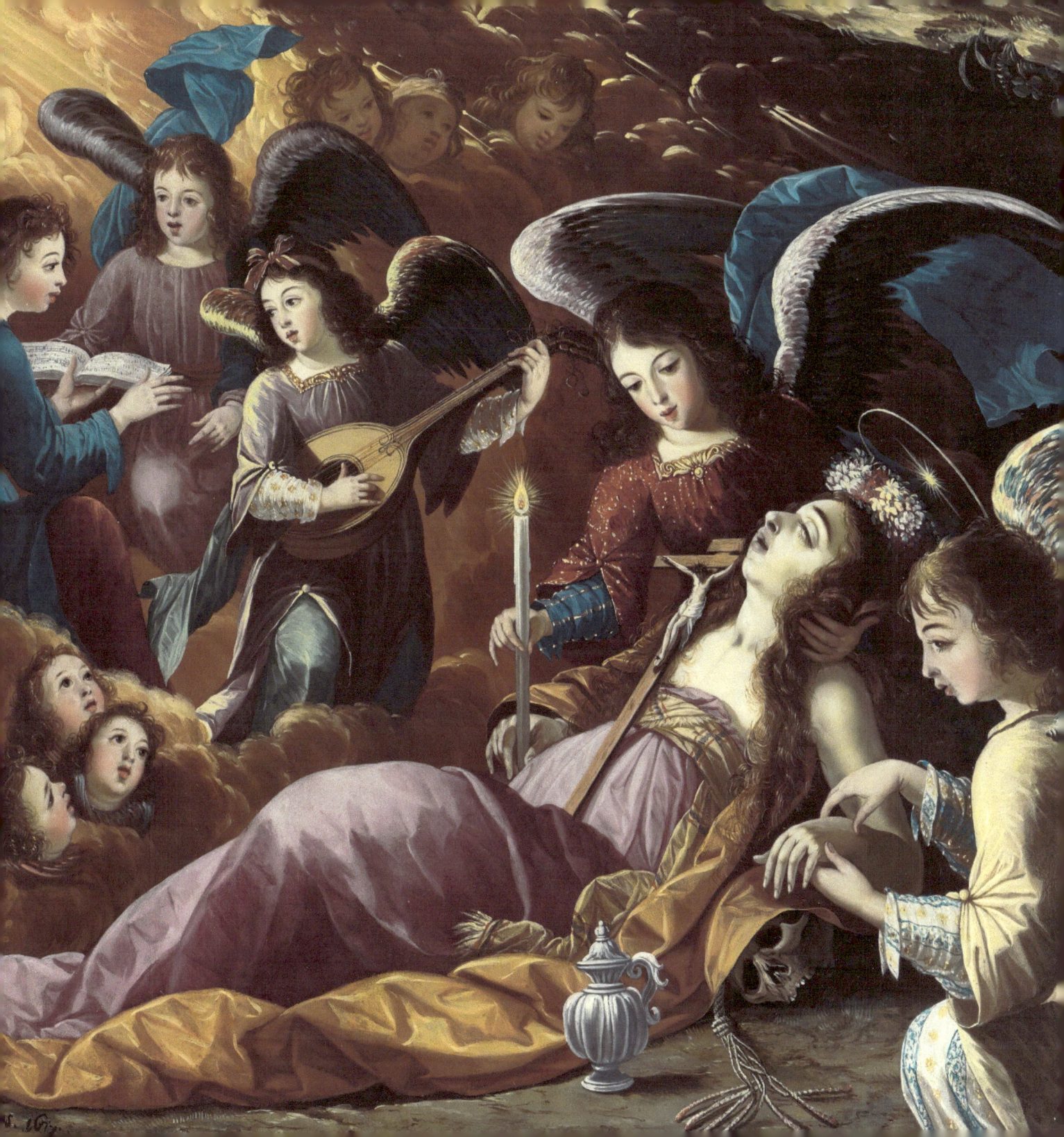

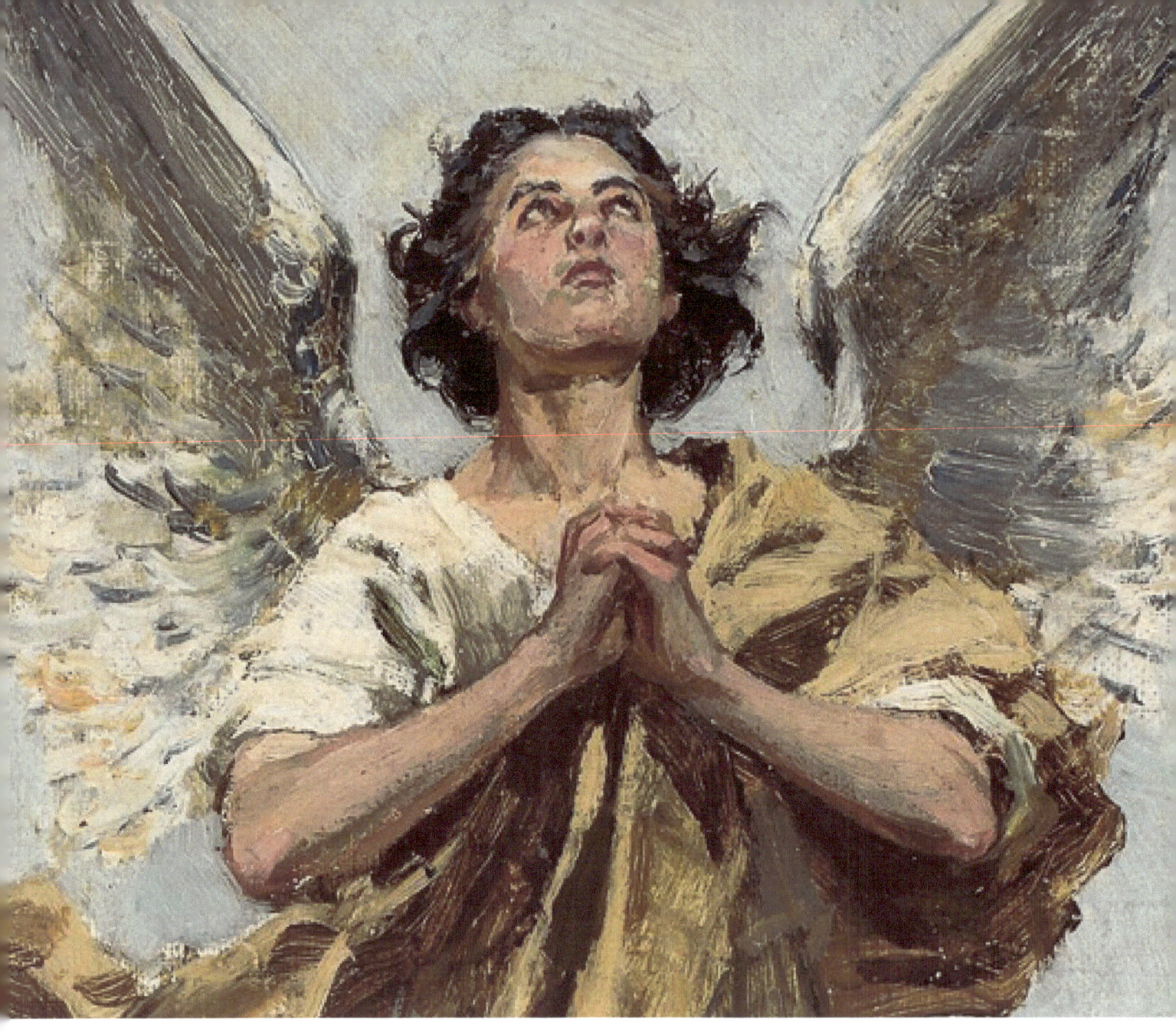

Angel
Tadeusz Popiel (Polish, 1863-1913)

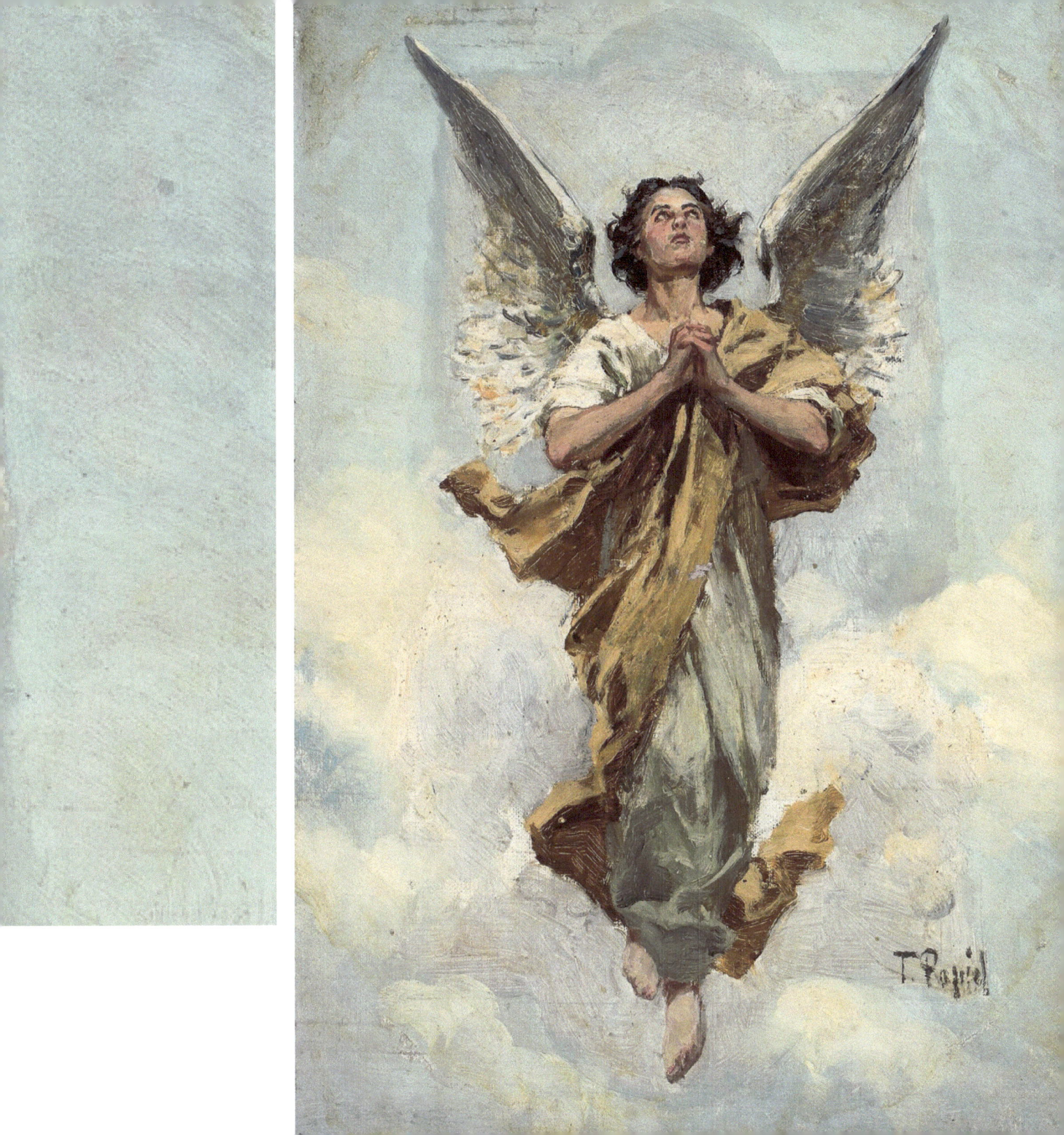

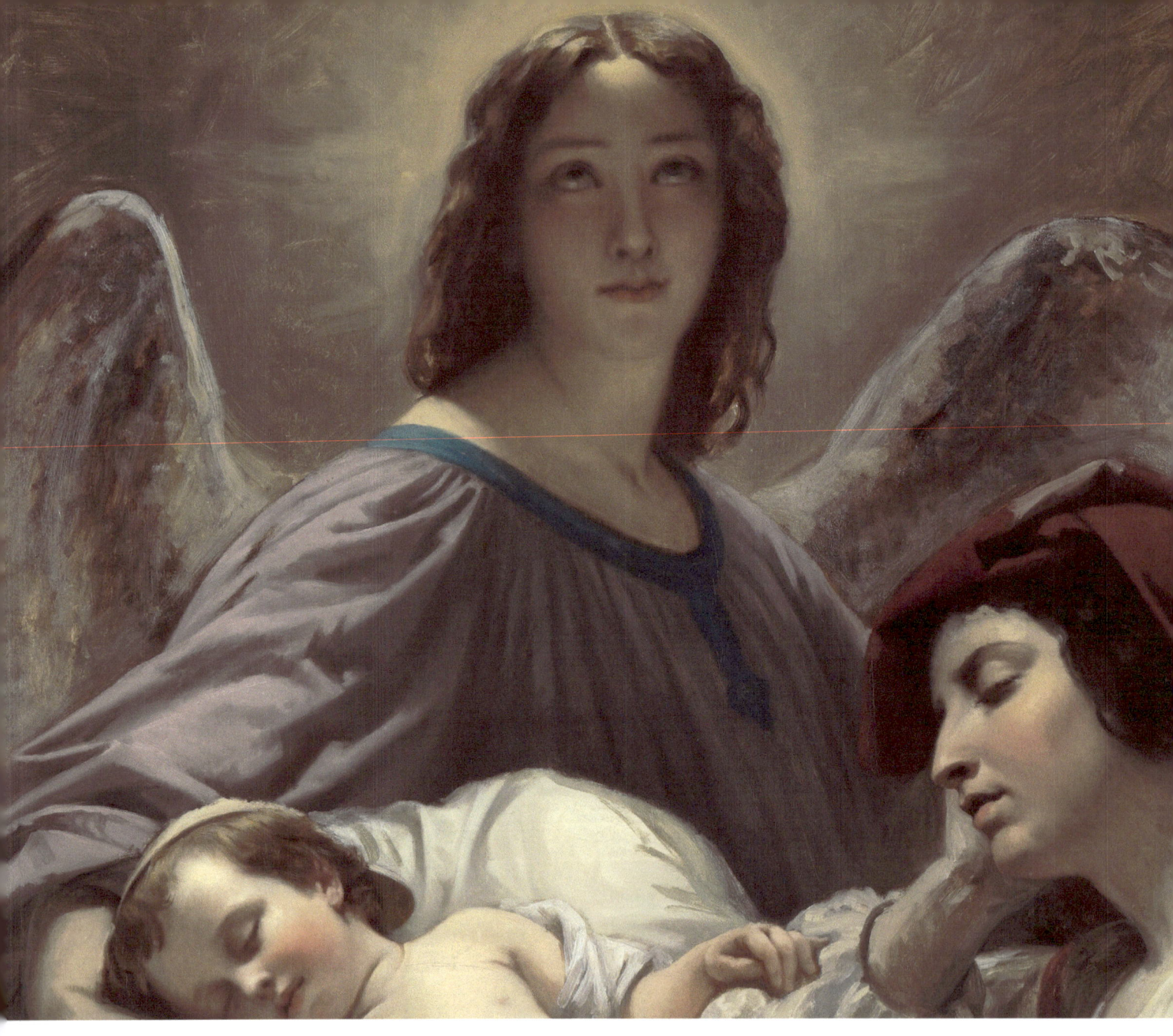

The Guardian Angel
Henri De Caisne (Belgian, 1799 – 1852)

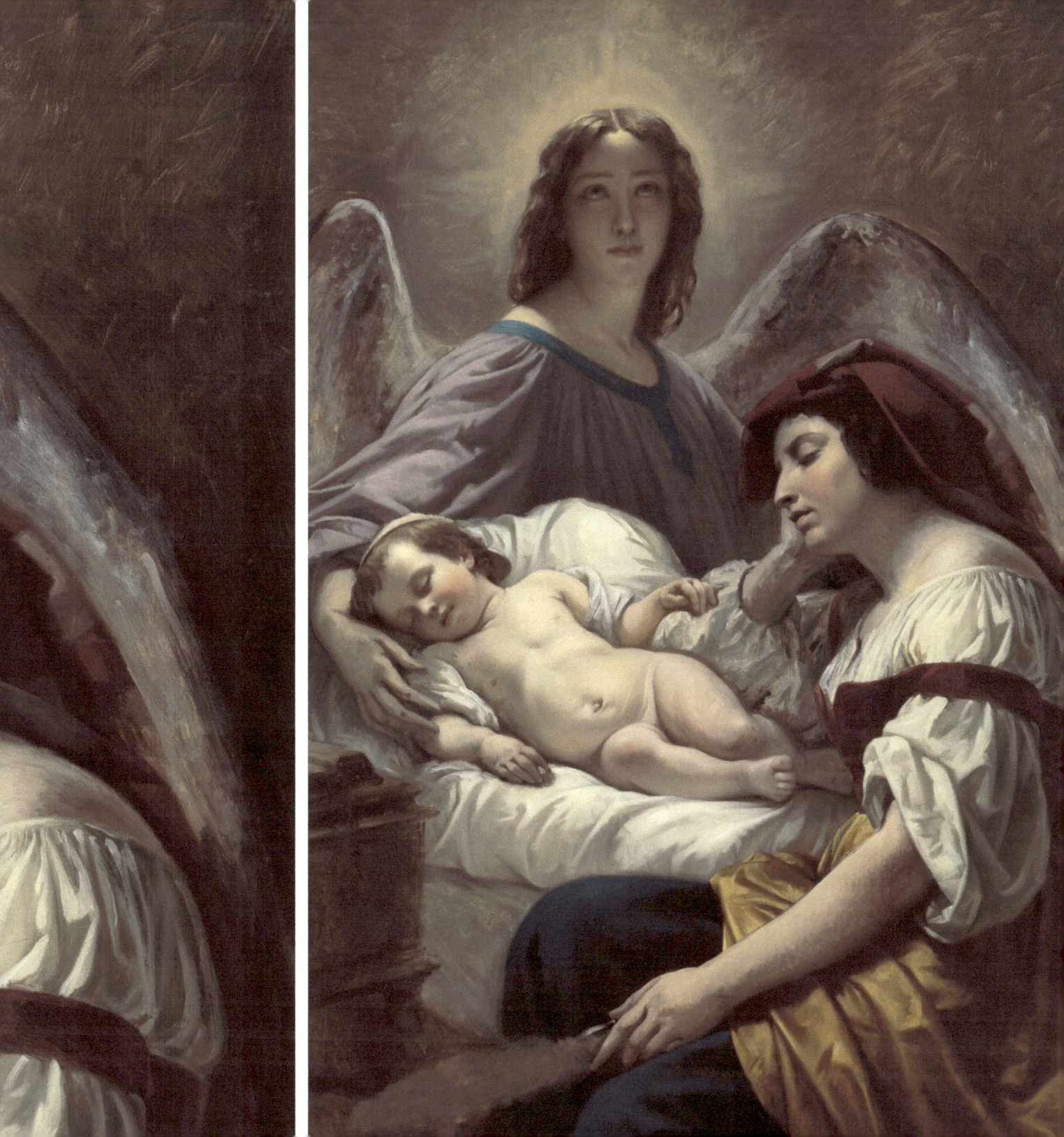

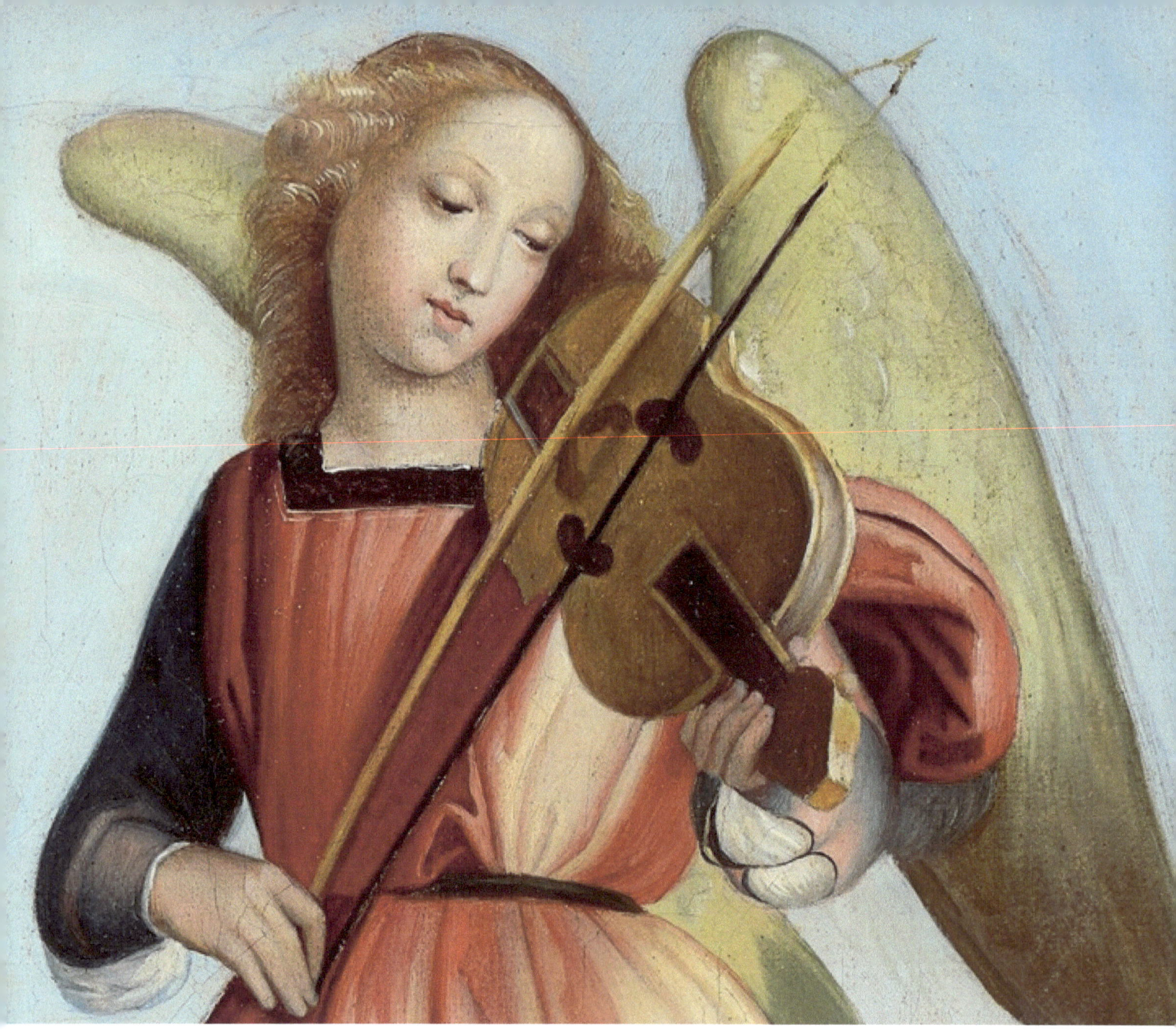

Music making angel (after Raffael)
Franz Ittenbach (German, 1813 - 1879)

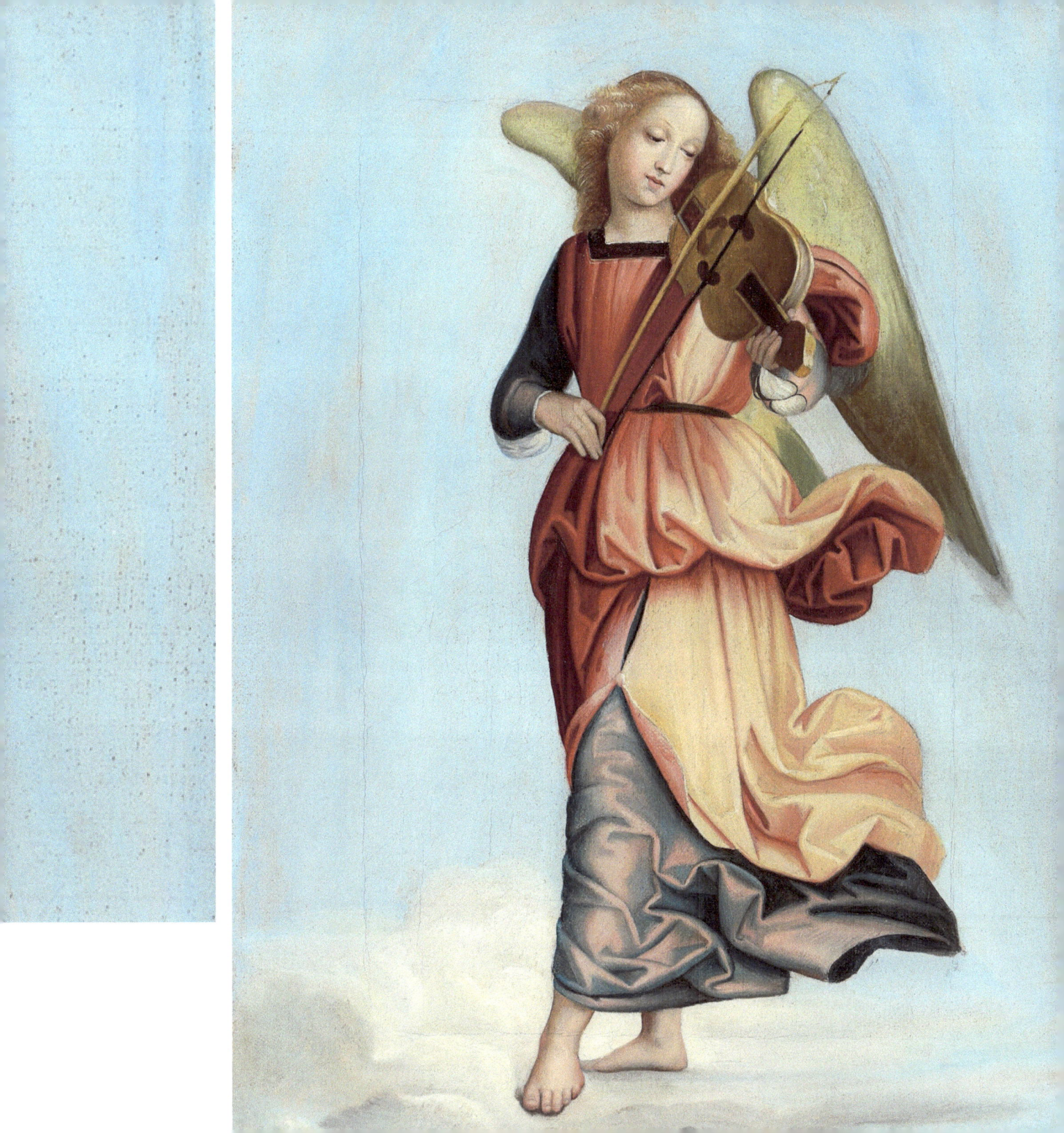

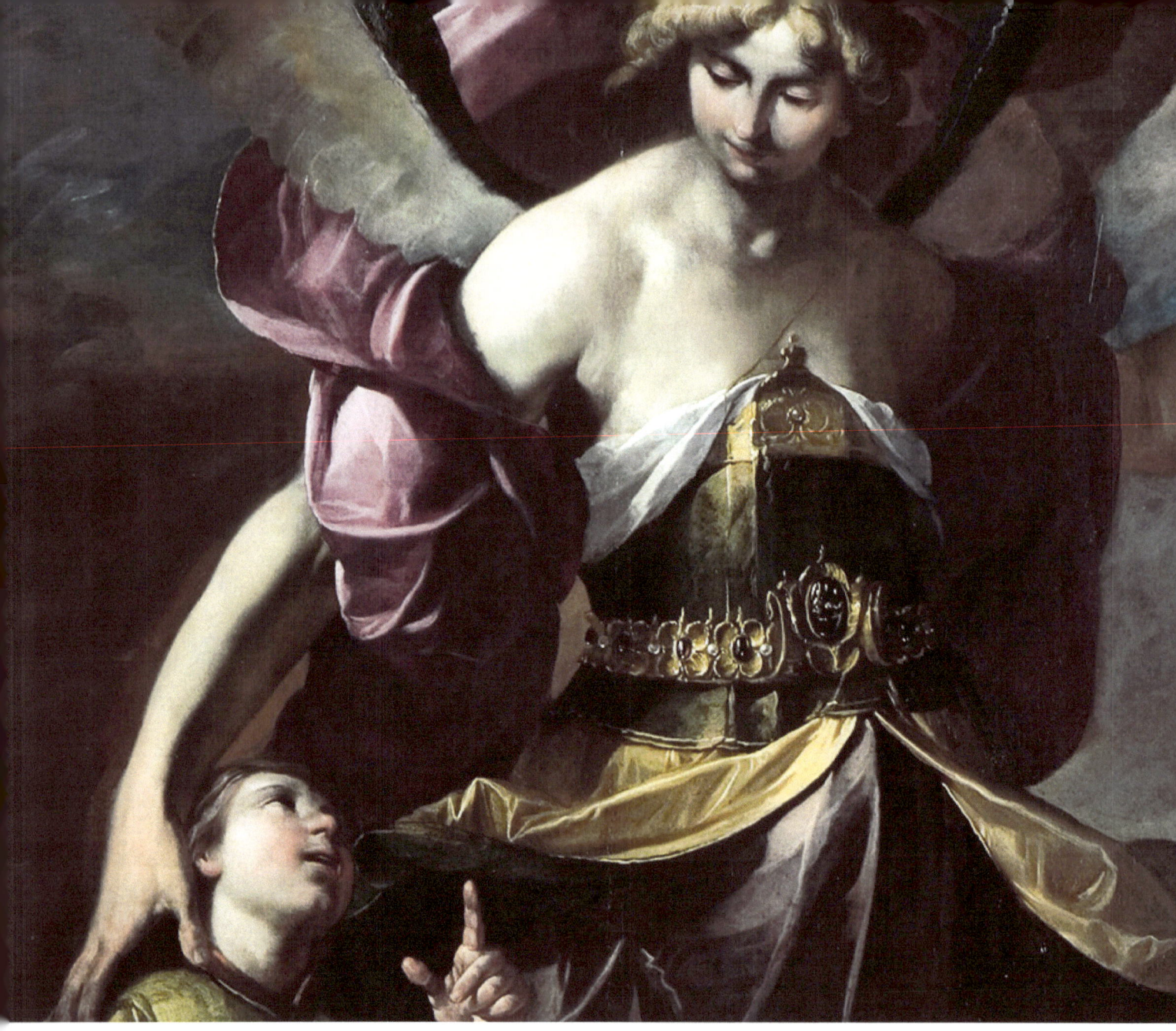

The Guardian Angel (1630)
Gioacchino Assereto (Italian, 1600 – 1649)

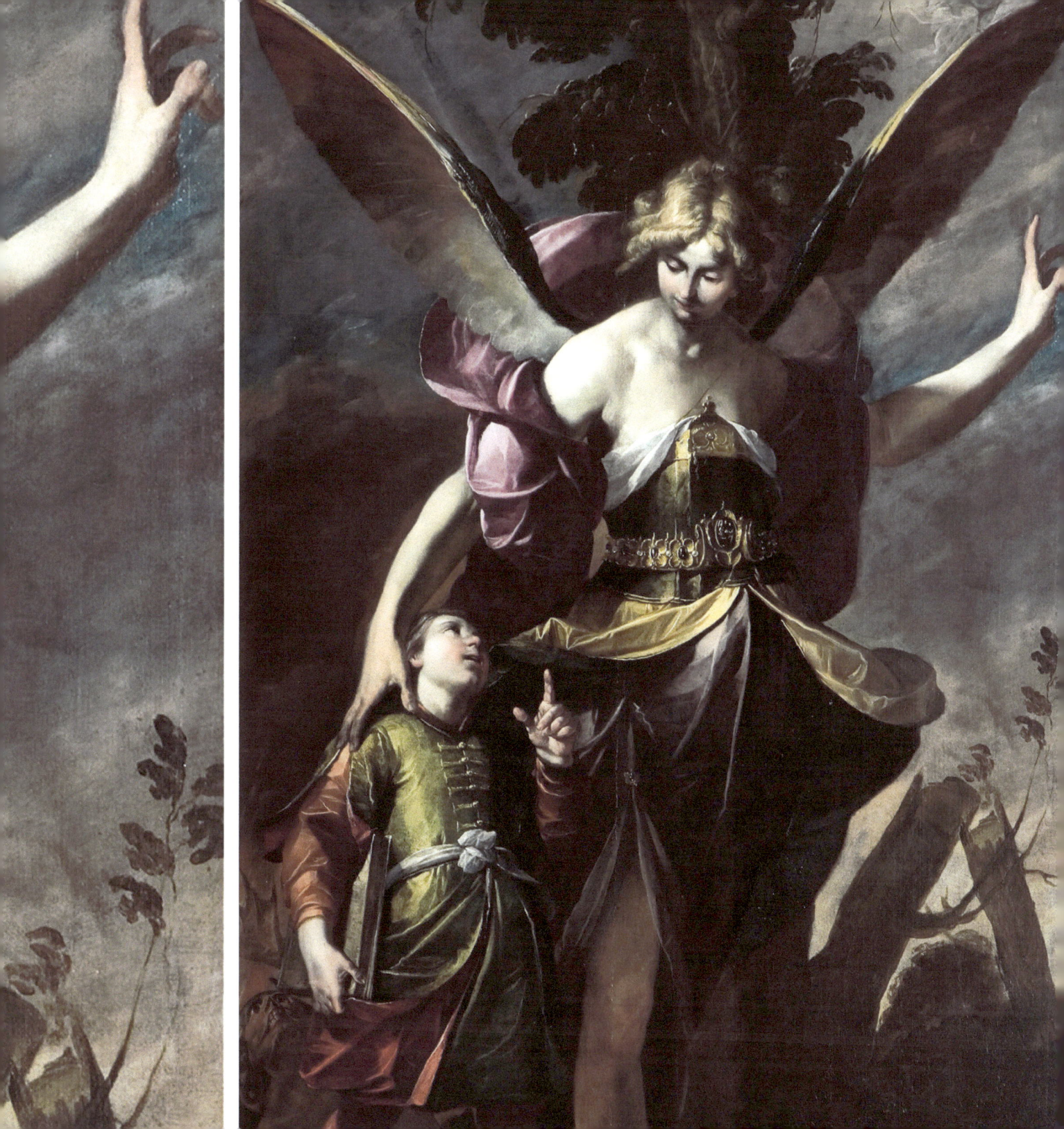

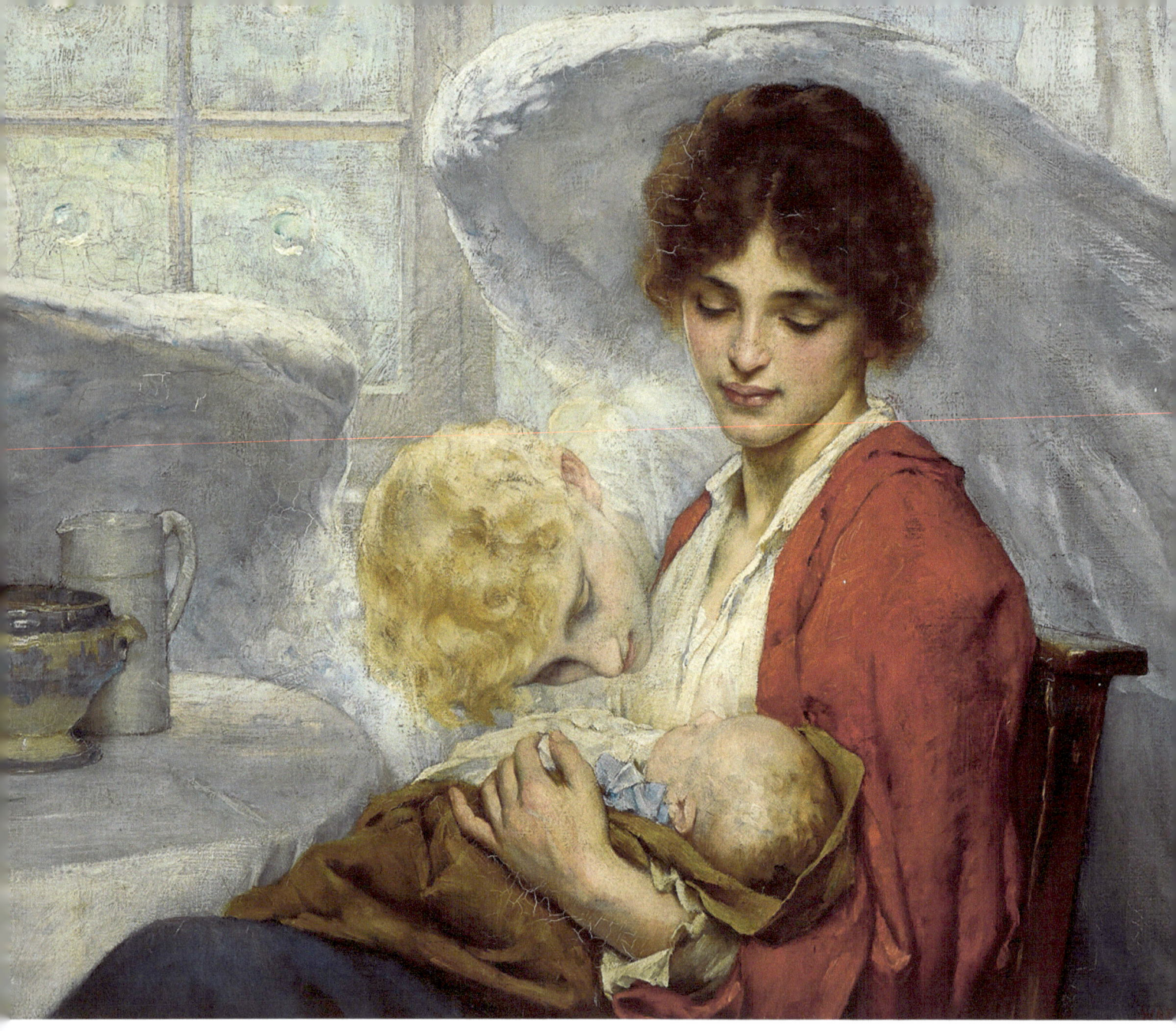

The Guardian Angel
William A. Breakspeare

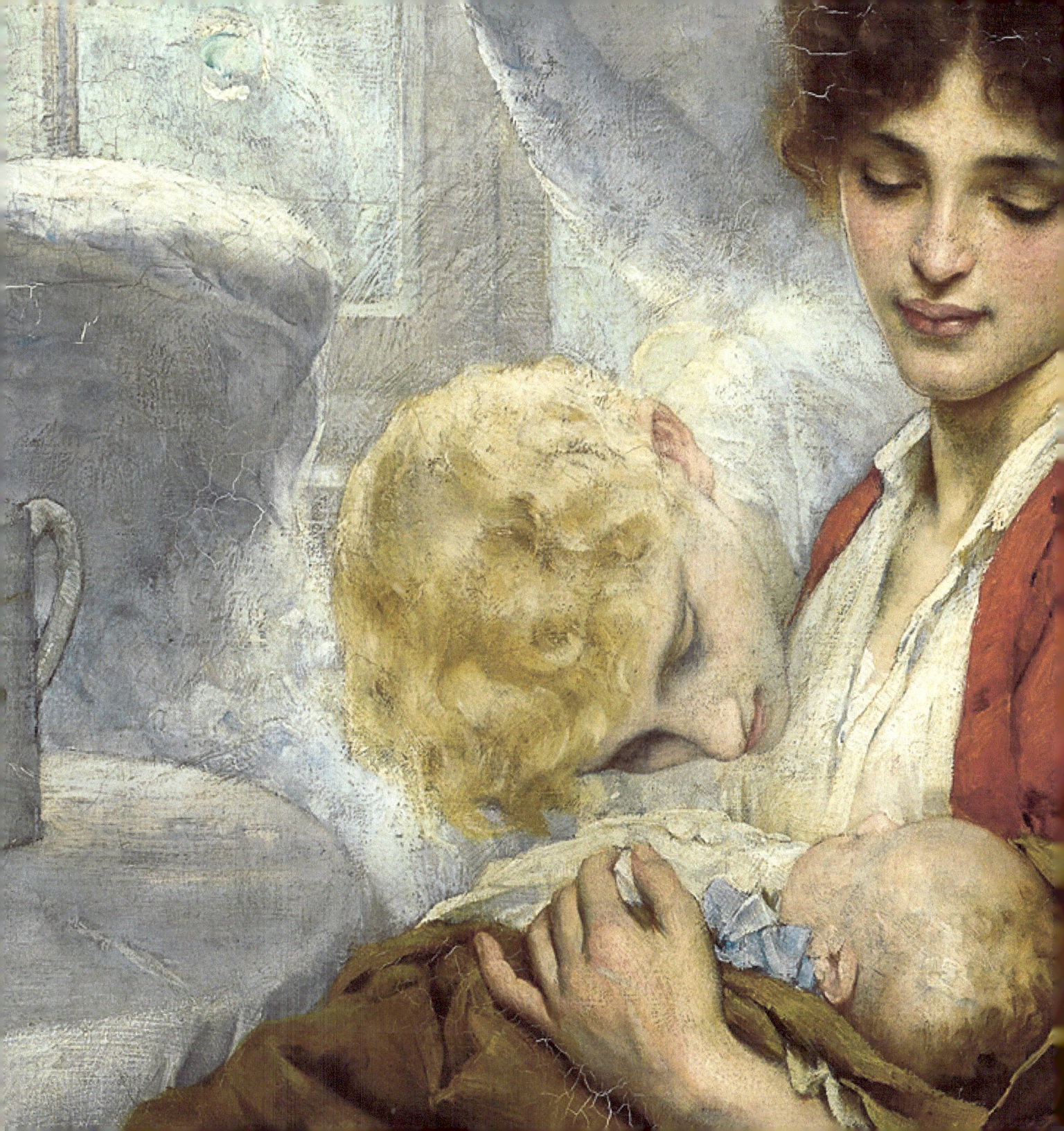

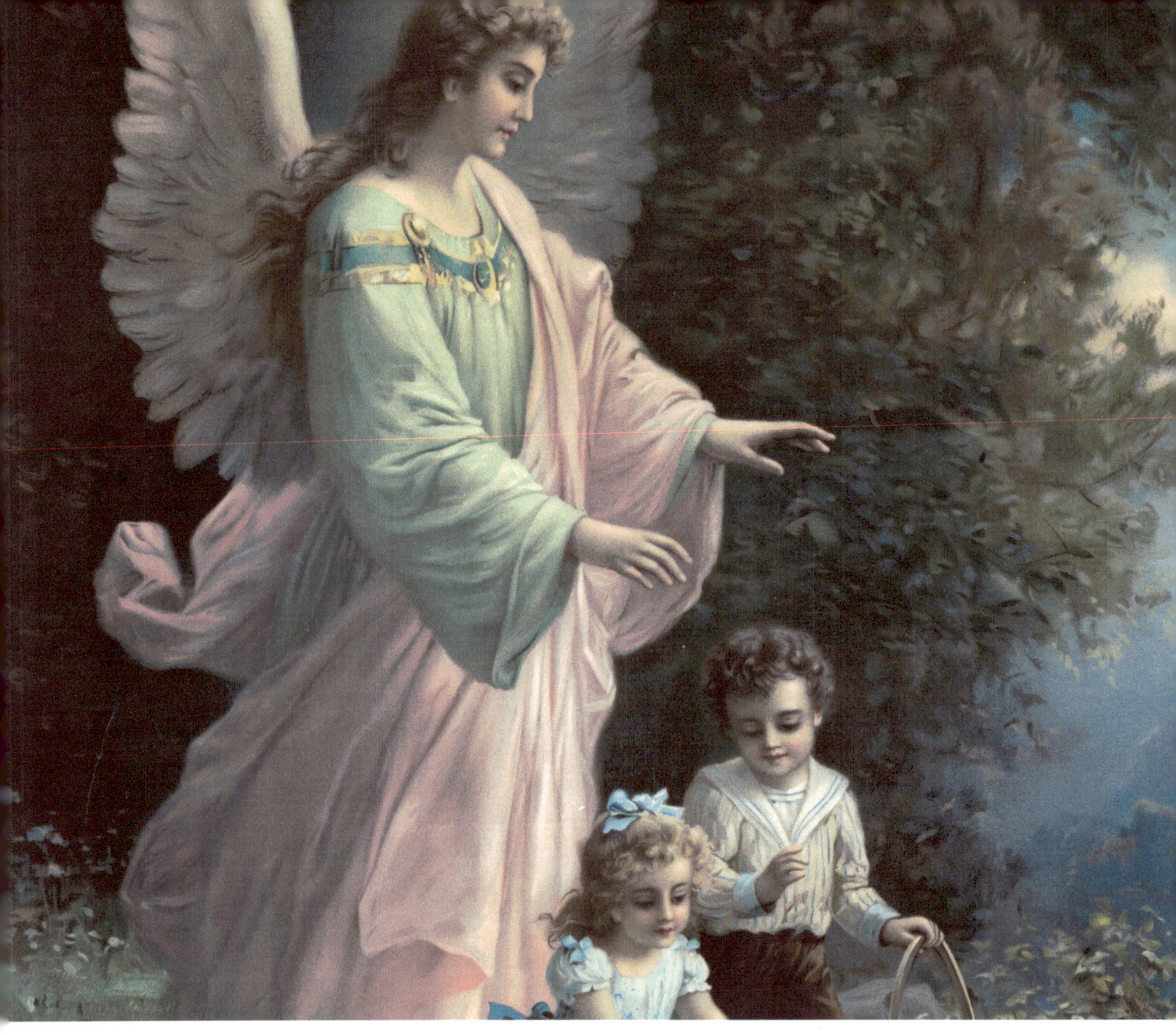

Guardian angel (1914)
Anonymous

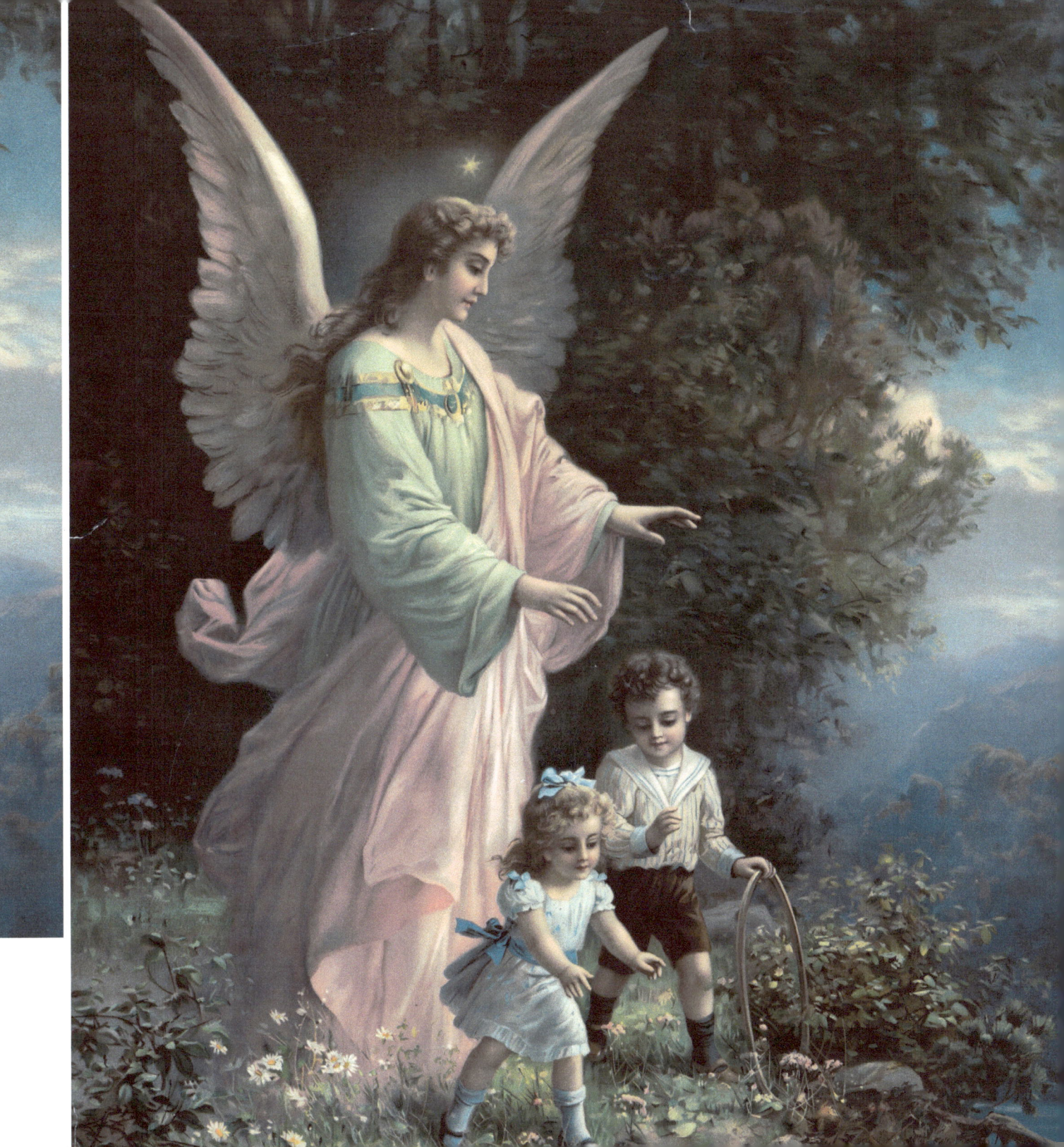

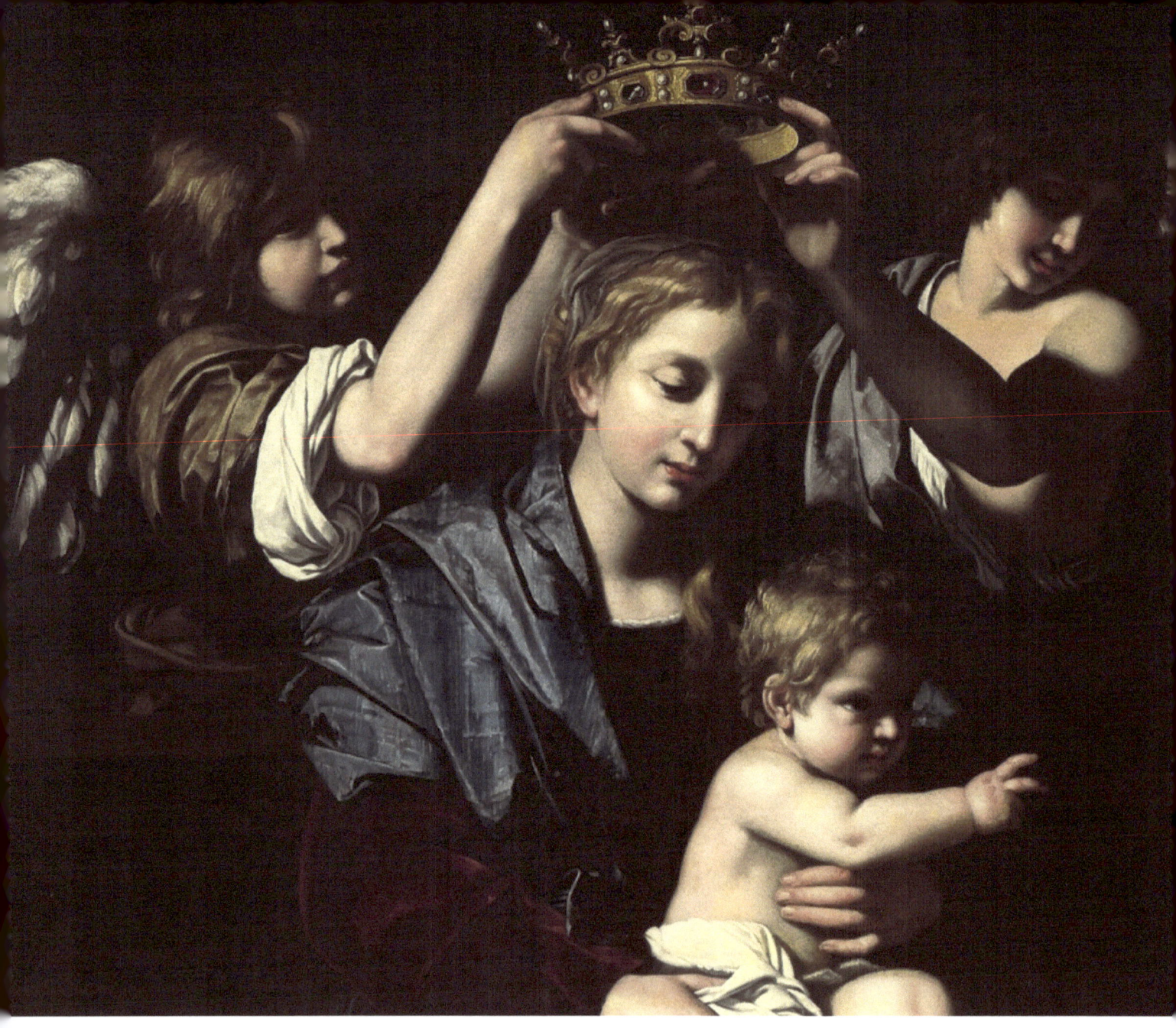

Virgin and Child with Angels (circa 1620)
Bartolomeo Cavarozzi (Italian, 1587-1625)

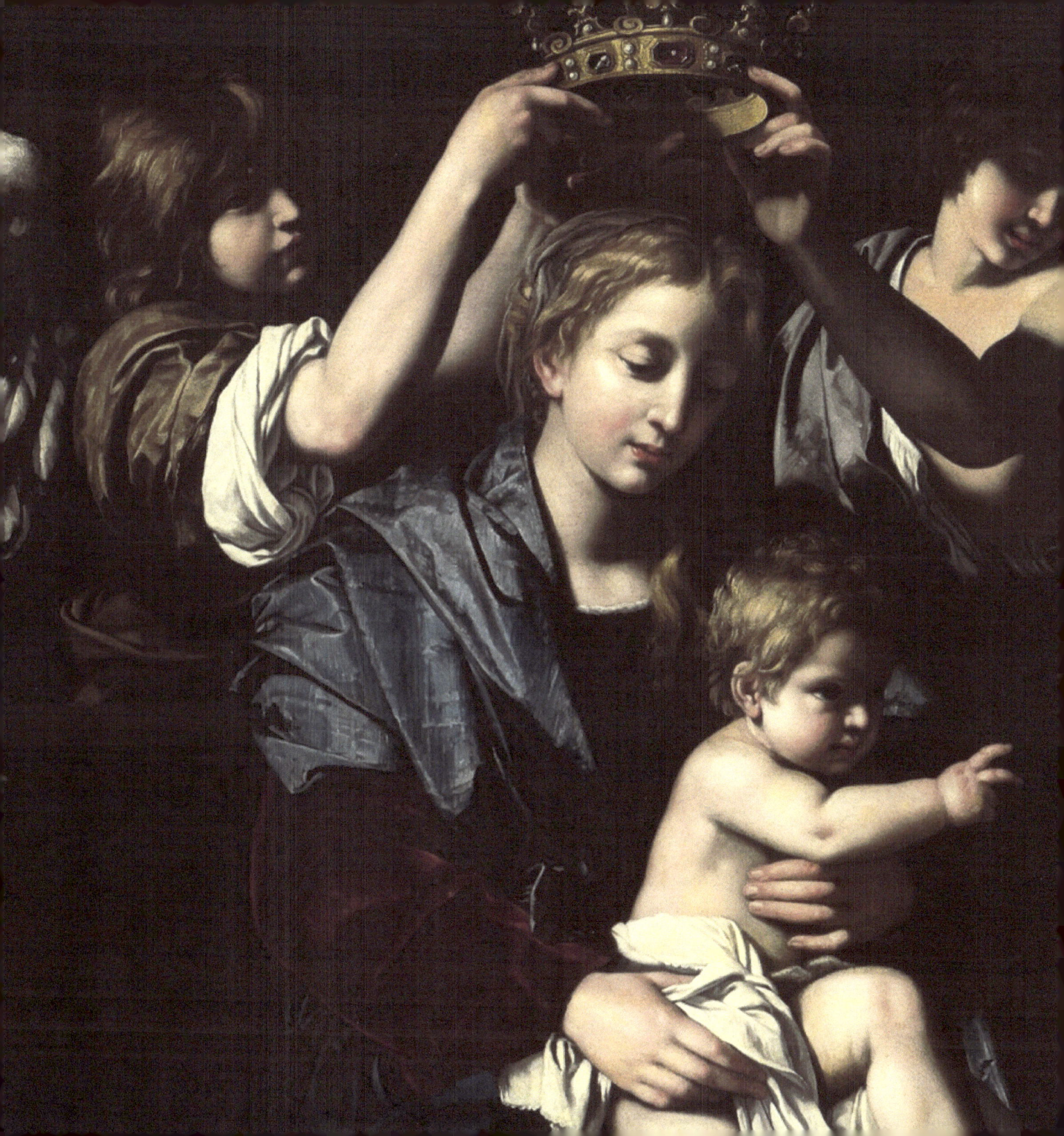